Policy Issues in Insurance

The Impact of the Financial Crisis on the Insurance Sector and Policy Responses

No. 13

This work is published on the responsibility of the Secretary-General of the OECD. The opinions expressed and arguments employed herein do not necessarily reflect the official views of the Organisation or of the governments of its member countries.

Please cite this publication as:
OECD (2011), *The Impact of the Financial Crisis on the Insurance Sector and Policy Responses No. 13*, OECD Publishing.
http://dx.doi.org/9789264092211-en

ISBN 978-92-64-09220-4 (print)
ISBN 978-92-64-09221-1 (PDF)

Series: Policy Issues in Insurance
ISSN 1990-083X (print)
ISSN 1990-0821 (online)

Corrigenda to OECD publications may be found on line at: *www.oecd.org/publishing/corrigenda*.
© OECD 2011

You can copy, download or print OECD content for your own use, and you can include excerpts from OECD publications, databases and multimedia products in your own documents, presentations, blogs, websites and teaching materials, provided that suitable acknowledgment of OECD as source and copyright owner is given. All requests for public or commercial use and translation rights should be submitted to *rights@oecd.org*. Requests for permission to photocopy portions of this material for public or commercial use shall be addressed directly to the Copyright Clearance Center (CCC) at *info@copyright.com* or the Centre français d'exploitation du droit de copie (CFC) at *contact@cfcopies.com*.

Foreword

Insurance markets play a key role in the pooling, management, and transfer of risks in the economy and, in some countries, increasingly play a role in the long-term savings and retirement incomes of individuals. The financial crisis highlighted the linkages of the insurance sector with the financial system and the broader economy.

This publication contains a report that sheds further light on the impact of the crisis on the insurance sector, building on an earlier OECD report examining the impact of the crisis on insurance companies.[1] The distinctive feature of this more recent report is that it is based on the results of a special questionnaire circulated within the OECD's Insurance and Private Pensions Committee in spring 2009. This questionnaire sought new data on the insurance sector – never before collected within the OECD – and information on policy and regulatory responses to the crisis.

The report shows that the insurance sector, overall, demonstrated resilience to the crisis, though with some variation across the OECD. In line with discussions within the Committee and as a means to promote reform, the report calls on OECD countries to enhance surveillance capacities and intervention tools, promote convergence to a common core regulatory framework for global insurers, ensure more comprehensive and consistent regulation across financial sectors, and promote financial education.

The Committee has, as a result of this report, decided to augment the OECD's statistical framework for insurance in order to enhance the surveillance capacities of the OECD and its member countries. Efforts will be made, in the coming years, to transform this statistical exercise into a global project extending beyond the OECD and make any necessary further improvements to the framework.

This publication has been prepared with technical support from Angélique Servin and Edward Smiley. A web-based version of this publication was released in April 2010.

[1.] See Sebastian Schich (2010), "Insurance Companies and the Financial Crisis", *Financial Market Trends* Vol. 2009/2, OECD, Paris.

Table of Contents

Introduction 7
    Notes 9

Impact of the Financial Turmoil 11
    Key balance sheet and investment indicators 11
    Premiums 22
    Claims 24
    Combined ratio 25
    Profitability 27
    Solvency 29
    Impact of the crisis on credit insurance markets 30
    Interpretation of statistical data 32
    Notes 33

Governmental and Supervisory Responses to the Crisis in the Insurance Sector 35
    Liquidity and short-term financing arrangements and the special case of AIG 36
    Capital levels and arrangements 38
    Corporate governance, risk management, investments, and reporting and disclosure ..40
    Insurance groups and financial conglomerates 41
    Policy holder protection schemes, restructuring and insolvency regimes 43
    Credit insurance markets 43
    Notes 46

Key Policy and Regulatory Issues in the Insurance Sector 49
    Notes 54

Key Policy Conclusions from the Crisis 55
    Notes 57

Annex A. Policy and Regulatory Responses to the Financial Crisis 59

Figures
    1. Total OECD GDP (volume) and GDP growth, 2007- Q3 of 2009 8
    2. Stock market developments, 2008-early 2010 8

3. Write-downs and credit losses in the banking and insurance sectors worldwide 12
4. Annual growth of industry assets by type of segment over 2007-2008
   in selected OECD countries 14
5. Direct insurers' asset allocation for selected investment categories by segments
   in selected OECD countries, 2008. As a percentage of total investments 15
6. Variation in equity allocations as a share of total portfolio investment,
   by segments, 2007-08 in selected OECD countries in percentage points 17
7. Breakdown of publicly traded vs. privately held equities for all segments
   in selected OECD countries, 2008 18
8. Corporate bond spreads, 1995 – early 2010 19
9. Share of public-sector and private-sector bonds for all segments in selected OECD
   countries, 2008. As a percentage of total industry bond investment 19
10. Average nominal net investment return by type of segment in selected OECD countries,
    in 2007 and 2008 21
11. 10-year Government benchmark bond yields, Jan. 2004 – Jan. 2010 22
12. Growth in life and non-life insurance net premiums written
    in selected OECD countries 2007-2008 23
13. Total life insurance gross premiums by type of contracts
    in selected OECD countries, 2008 24
14. Growth in total gross claim payments in selected OECD countries, 2007-2008 25
15. Non-life combined ratio in selected OECD countries, 2007-2008 26
16. Non-life loss ratio in selected OECD countries, 2007-2008 26
17. Return on assets (ROA) by type of segment in selected OECD countries, 2008 27
18. Return on equity (ROE) by type of segment in selected OECD countries, 2008 28
19. Change in equity position (2007-2008) 28

Tables

1. Write-downs, credit losses and capital raised by major insurance companies 12
2. Solvency margin by type of segment in selected OECD and non-OECD countries 29
3. Asset valuation methodologies across countries 32
A.1. Liquidity or lending support 60
A.2. Capital levels and injections 62
A.3. Corporate governance and risk management, investments, and reporting,
     disclosure and transparency 67
A.4. Insurance groups and financial conglomerates 73
A.5. Policy holder protection schemes, and restructuring and insolvency regime 77
A.6. Regulatory regime and process 81
A.7. Intervention in credit insurance markets 84

Introduction

The financial turmoil, which started with the sub-prime mortgage crisis in the United States and whose effects clearly became global in mid-2007 with the collapse of several large international hedge funds and the near-collapse of a major industrial bank in Germany, followed by the breakdown of interbank lending markets in August 2007, has had important, continued impacts on the economy, including the insurance sector. Events took a turn for the worse when, during the second half of 2008, the crisis exploded into a global credit crunch following the collapse of major global financial institutions. The ensuing recession officially became, by April 2009, the second longest since the Great Depression. Following a fall of 2.1% in the first quarter of 2009, gross domestic product in the OECD area stabilised in the second and third quarters according to preliminary estimates (see Figure 1).

Stock market valuations fell dramatically following the severe aggravation of the financial crisis in September and October 2008 (see Figure 2). However, in March 2009, markets began to rally. Between March and end-January 2010, stock indices1 rose by more than 35% for the United States and more than 40% for the Euro area. Even though some softening has been evident since October 2009, the deterioration in equity performance has nonetheless impacted insurers. That said, and as to be explained more fully below, other factors have had an important impact on the financial condition of insurers, such as widening credit spreads and a lower yield environment for risk-free debt instruments.

After exhibiting several years of strong returns on equity and balance sheet growth, insurers started facing balance-sheet challenges in 2008. The slump in investment performance, with associated increased amounts of (un)realised losses reflecting mark-to-market accounting practices, eroded insurers' equity positions. Many companies also started to feel the impact of credit-spread widening on profitability in 2008. Corporate spreads have since improved, which should support profitability.

Deteriorating economic conditions and rising corporate insolvencies resulting from the financial crisis have led to worsened conditions for some lines of insurance business, most notably director and officer liability and trade credit insurance. Trade credit insurance has been particularly hard hit, with retrenchment by insurers in this sector affecting business transactions and bank lending, further aggravating the business environment.

Going forward, a number of key parameters will determine the continued impact of the financial turmoil on the insurance sector – namely, the credit and interest rate environment, equity market performance, and the strength of the real economy. Continued monitoring of the insurance sector is therefore warranted.[2]

8 - INTRODUCTION

Figure 1. **Total OECD GDP (volume) and GDP growth, 2007- Q3 of 2009**

2000 = 100, seasonally adjusted

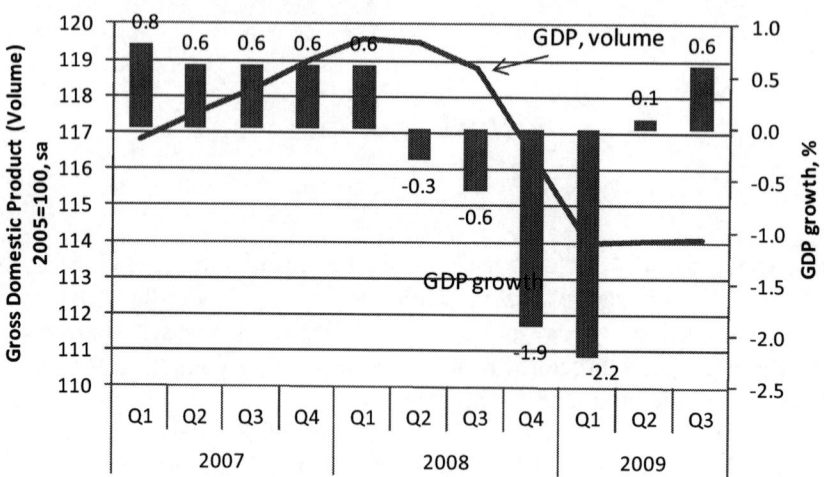

Source: OECD Quarterly National Accounts.

Figure 2. **Stock market developments, 2008-early 2010**

Datastream total market price index (1/1/2008=100)

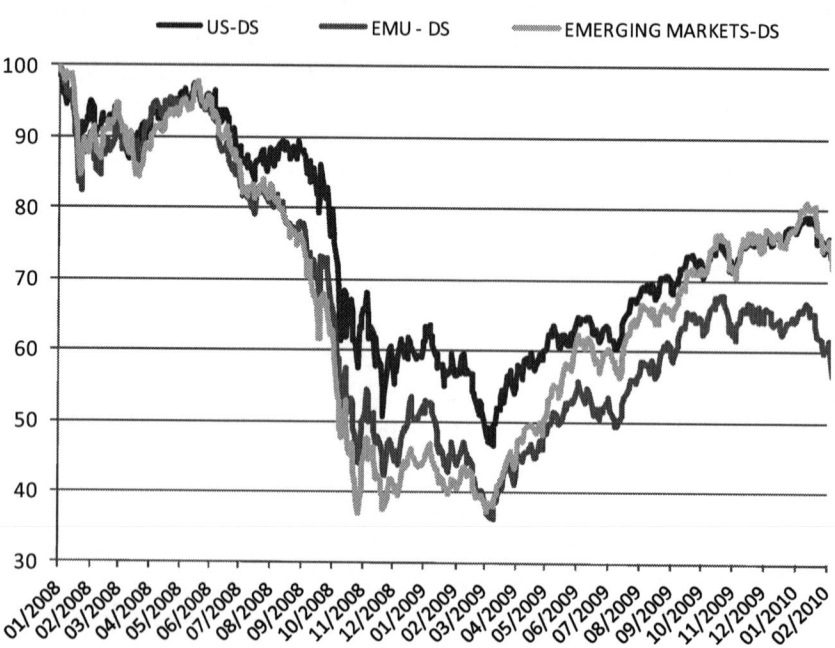

Note: "US-DS total market", "EMU-DS" and "EMERGING MARKETS-DS total market" are market indexes calculated by Datastream (DS) for the U.S., European Monetary Union, and emerging markets, respectively.
Source: Thomson Reuters Datastream.

Notes

1. Based on Datastream total stock market price indices.

2. This report was elaborated within the OECD Insurance and Private Pensions Committee in 2009 and was approved by the Committee for publication. The report contributes to the OECD's *Strategic Response to the Financial and Economic Crisis* (see *www.oecd.org/crisisresponse*). The information in this report draws largely on information collected from OECD member countries in response to a special fast-track questionnaire on the impact of the financial crisis on the insurance sector that was circulated as well as on Committee discussions. The report was prepared by Timothy Bishop and Jean-Marc Salou of the OECD Secretariat.

Impact of the Financial Turmoil

The insurance sector played an important supporting role in the financial crisis by virtue of the role played by financial guarantee insurance in wrapping, and elevating the credit standing of, complex structured products and thus making these products more attractive to investors and globally ubiquitous.[1] In addition, the narrowly avoided collapse of AIG Incorporated (AIG Inc.), viewed by some as the world's largest insurance group consisting of a global financial service holding company with 71 U.S. based insurance companies and 176 other financial service companies, contributed to the severity of the market turmoil in September 2008. Furthermore, growing corporate insolvencies and a negative credit watch outlook caused important dislocation and retrenchment in trade credit insurance markets, which added considerable stress to business-to-business transactions and increased liquidity pressures on firms in an already liquidity-stressed environment, and thus aggravating the effects of the economic crisis.

However, in general, the traditional life and general insurance sectors have largely been bystanders in the crisis, and have been impacted by its knock-on effects, such as the fall in equity markets, declines in interest rates, economic slowdown and decline in credit quality, and, in some cases, counterparty exposures to failed financial institutions. In some respects, aside from the financial guarantee insurance lines that amplified downward pressures in financial markets,[2] and adjustments in trade credit insurance lines that have added stress to business transactions with attendant economic impacts,[3] the insurance sector has arguably helped to provide a stabilising influence in light of its longer-term investment horizon and conservative investment approach.

Key balance sheet and investment indicators

Generally limited direct exposure to toxic assets

A main channel through which insurance undertakings were affected by the market turmoil was via their asset side investments in equity and debt instruments as well as structured finance products. In terms of direct impact of the crisis, the exposure of insurance undertakings to sub-prime mortgages and related "toxic" assets such as collateralised debt obligations (CDOs) and structured investment vehicles (SIVs), which initiated the current financial crisis, does not appear to have been significant in most OECD countries on the basis of the limited data that has become available. This result appears to reflect, in large part, conservative investment strategies and, to some extent, regulatory requirements such as diversification rules and limitations on investments in alternative investment vehicles.

That said, in some specific OECD countries, certain (re)insurers (particularly life insurers) have had important exposures to sub-prime mortgage and "toxic" products and have therefore had to write down the value of their holdings and recognise material losses (as impairments or unrealised mark-to-market value losses) as the markets for these products collapsed. Based on aggregated data from Bloomberg, as of January 2010, insurers worldwide have reported write-downs and credit losses of USD 261 billion, compared with USD 1 230 billion in the banking sector. In Europe, the insurance sector reported USD 69 billion of write-downs and credit losses, while the comparable amount for the US is USD 189 billion. As of January 2010, four major insurance groups accounted for 54% of all write-downs worldwide, namely, AIG, ING Groep N.V., Ambac Financial Group Inc and Aegon NV, that recorded write-downs valued at USD 98.2 billion, USD 18.6 billion, USD 12.0 billion and USD 10.7 billion respectively (see Table 1).

Figure 3. **Write-downs and credit losses in the banking and insurance sectors worldwide**

USD billion (as of January 2010)

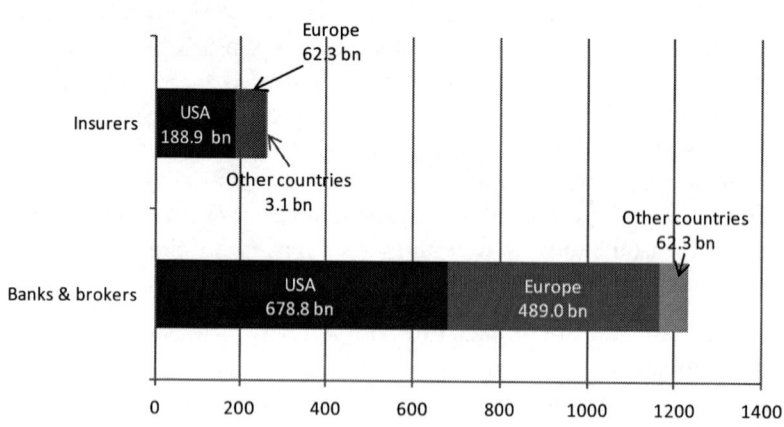

Source: Bloomberg.

Table 1. **Write-downs, credit losses and capital raised by major insurance companies**

Total since 2007, in USD billion (as of January 2010)

Insurance companies	Writedown & Loss	Capital Raised	Shortfall
American International Group (AIG)	98.2	98.1	-0.1
ING Groep N.V.	18.6	24.1	5.5
Ambac Financial Group Inc	12.0	1.4	-10.6
Aegon NV	10.7	4.0	-6.7
Hartford Financial SVCS GRP	9.7	6.4	-3.3
Fortis	9.3	22.7	13.4
Swiss Re	8.5	2.9	-5.6
Metlife Inc	7.2	4.0	-3.2
Allianz SE	7.0	2.0	-5.0
Allstate Corp	6.6	0.0	-6.6
Prudential Financial Inc	6.6	5.9	-0.7
MBIA Inc	5.7	1.0	-4.7
Aflac Inc	5.2	0.0	-5.2
Genworth Financial Inc-CL A	4.8	0.6	-4.2
XL Capital	4.0	2.6	-1.4
CNA Financial Corp	3.1	1.2	-1.9
Zurich Financial	3.1	0.0	-3.1
Other	40.7	14.8	-25.9
Total	261.0	191.7	-69.3
memo item: total US	188.9	127.4	-61.5
memo item: total European	69.0	59.9	-9.1

Source: Bloomberg.

The indirect effects of the crisis – involving large declines in world equity markets from October 2008 to March 2009, changes in corporate spreads and risk-free rates, and developments in the real economy – have been moderate in their impact on the insurance sector but nonetheless became more pronounced in 2008 since the outbreak of the crisis in 2007. These are discussed below.

Balance sheet and investment portfolio trends

In a healthy market environment, it can be expected that industry assets will grow due to continued receipt of premium income, positive reinvested investment returns, stable dividends and share repurchases, debt and share issuance, and, if equity markets are favourable, positive changes in the value of assets. However, in the context of the crisis, the growth in total industry assets of insurance undertakings in OECD insurance markets (for which 2008 data was available) was mixed in 2008. As shown in Figure 4, in nine countries (out of seventeen for which such data was available) total life industry assets fell. Within this category, Australia, Belgium, Finland, Germany and the United States showed the largest drop – in the range of -8% to -50% – with Australia and Belgium reporting the highest decrease in assets in the life segment, down by 14% and 50% respectively in 2008. By contrast, total life industry assets grew exceptionally strongly in Turkey,[4] and strong growth was recorded in Poland and Mexico.

In the non-life sector, the pattern is of more generalised positive growth in industry assets, with only six countries (out of eighteen for which such data was available) experiencing a decrease in their non-life assets. Asset growth was positive or flat for composite undertakings in eight of the nine countries that have provided information.[5]

Generally limited allocation to equity has helped to protect insurers from market volatility

Equity holdings in investment portfolios have been a channel through which the financial turmoil affected insurers and brought about a fall in the value of portfolio holdings. However, this transmission channel appears to have generally been limited for insurers, as equity holdings in many OECD countries do not make up a dominant proportion of insurers' overall investment portfolios, reflecting a downward trend in equity ownership in recent years; that said, there may be cases of insurers within these jurisdictions that have higher equity exposures and thus may have been adversely impacted by equity market declines.

As shown in Figure 5, in most OECD countries that provided information for 2008, bonds – not equity – remain by far the dominant asset class across life, non-life and composite insurance segments, accounting respectively for 67%, 62% and 74%, suggesting an overall conservative stance.[6] There are also OECD countries like Austria, Finland, France, Italy, the Netherlands and Poland that showed significant portfolio allocations to equities, in the range of 23% to 38%.

Figure 4. **Annual growth of industry assets by type of segment over 2007-2008 in selected OECD countries**

Percentage

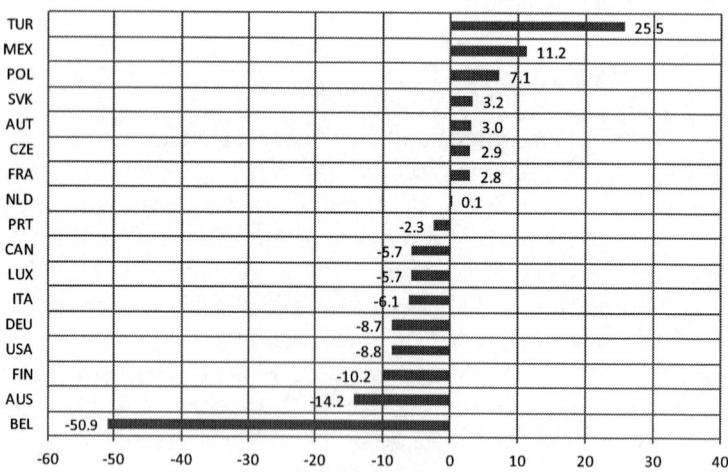

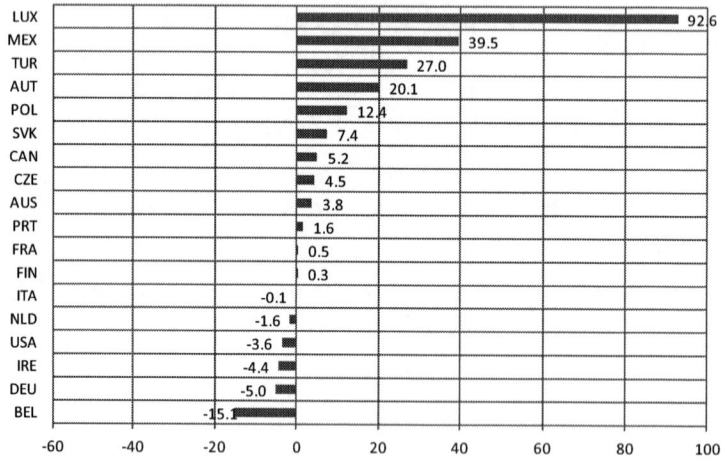

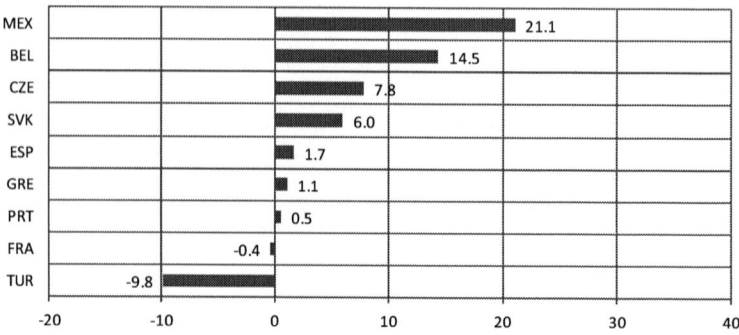

Note: Life segment includes unit-linked.
Source: OECD Insurance Statistics.

There seems to be a consistent investment pattern among life and non-life undertakings across OECD countries. For most of the countries for which such data was available, life insurance undertakings invest more heavily in bonds than non-life undertakings, respectively 69% and 61% on average (simple average). With respect to investments in shares, non-life undertakings invested on average 15% of their investments in this asset class as opposed to 8% for life insurance undertakings. For example, in Italy, 38.4% of the total non-life portfolio was invested in shares in 2008, as compared to 10.5% of the total life portfolio. Yet, the reverse situation exists (*i.e.*, greater investment in shares by life insurance undertakings when compared to non-life undertakings) in Belgium, Canada, the Czech Republic and Finland.

In almost all OECD countries for which such data was available, the weight of equities in portfolios decreased from 2007 to 2008, or increased only marginally (see Figure 6). This may be due to real rebalancing or to a decrease in the weight of equity in the total portfolio owing to the fall in equity prices.

Figure 5. **Direct insurers' asset allocation for selected investment categories by segments in selected OECD countries[7], 2008**

As a percentage of total investments

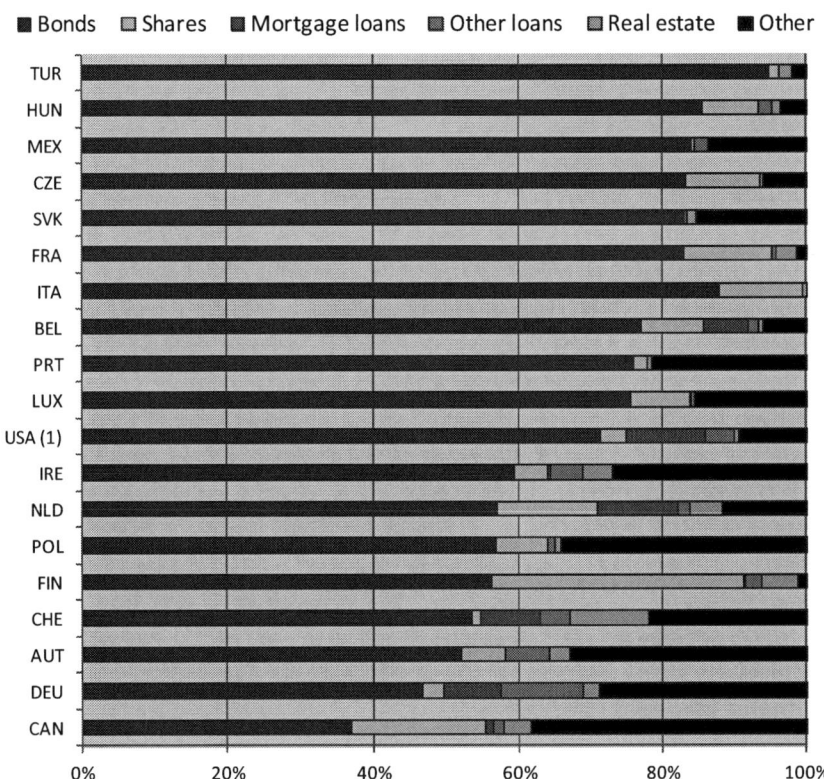

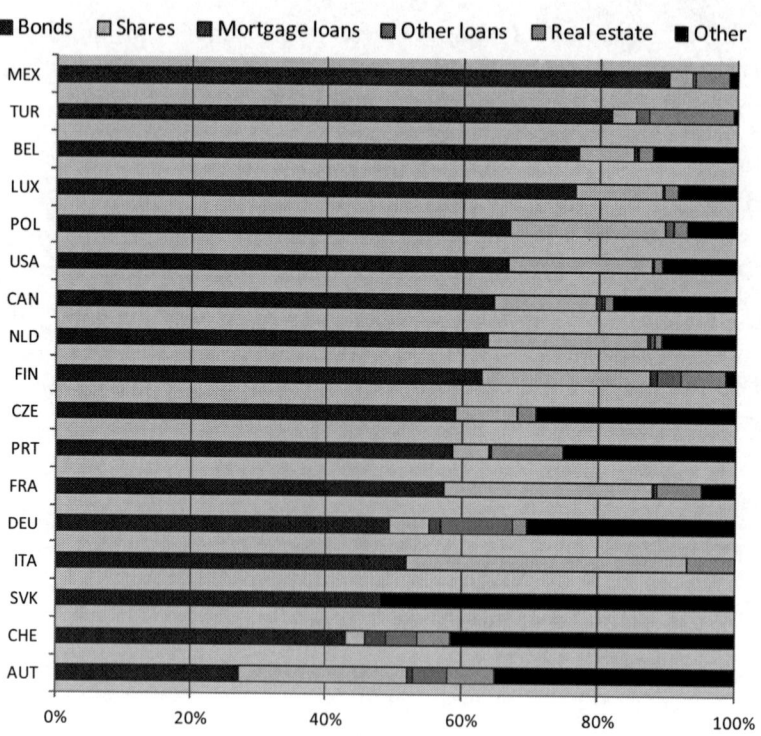

Note: The category of investment identified as 'Other' includes primarily cash, deposits and to a much less extent alternative investments (hedge funds, private equity, and commodities, among others).
(1) "Bonds" includes only long-term bonds. Short-term debt investments are included in "other investments".
Source: OECD Insurance Statistics.

The important role of equity investments in privately held equities in some OECD countries

Six OECD countries out of eleven for which such data was available displayed a share of privately held equities equal or more than half of total equities held by insurers (see Figure 7). This asset class, not traded on an active market, is valued at book value in certain jurisdictions (*e.g.*, Portugal). In the case of long-term assets such as investments in other companies, the book value does not reflect the actual value. Should the value of the company's stock increase over time, the value of the asset remains hidden until the shares of equity are sold and an actual cash flow is realised.

Figure 6. **Variation in equity allocations as a share of total portfolio investment, by segments, 2007-08 in selected OECD countries**[8]

in percentage points

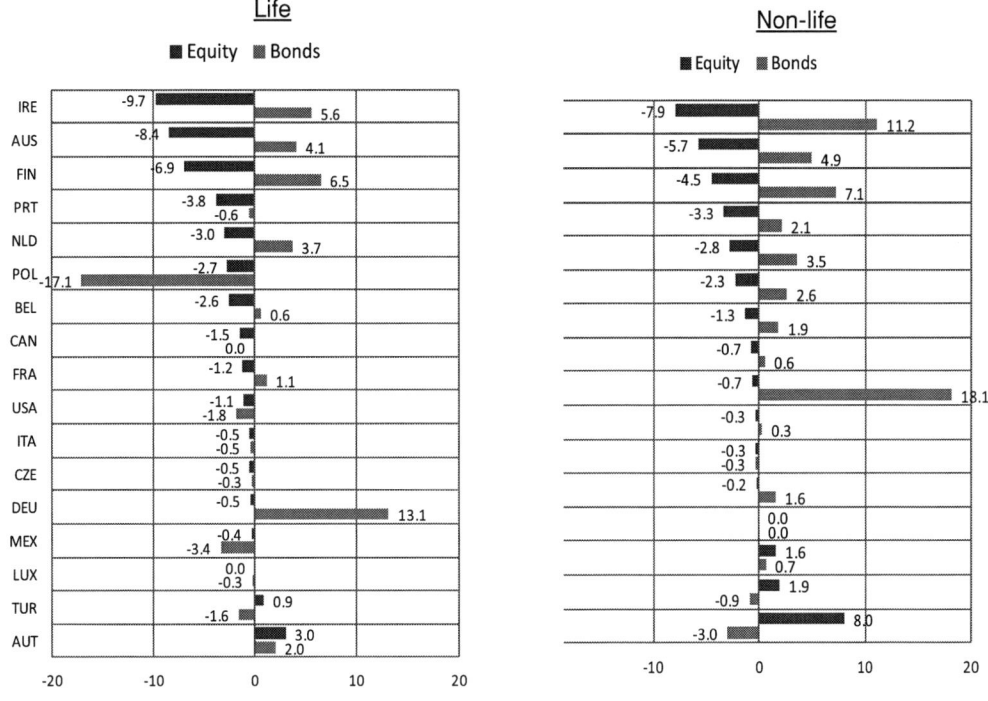

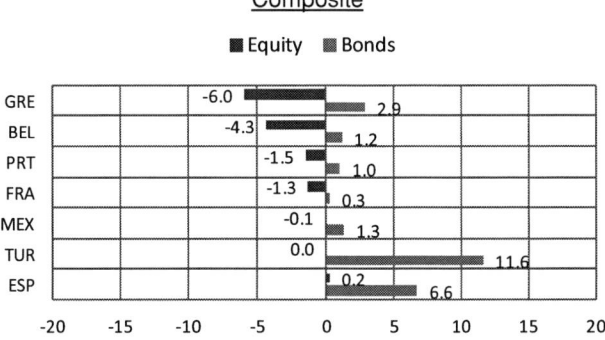

Note: Data refer to direct insurance only.
Source: OECD Insurance Statistics.

Figure 7. **Breakdown of publicly traded vs. privately held equities for all segments[9] in selected OECD countries, 2008[10]**

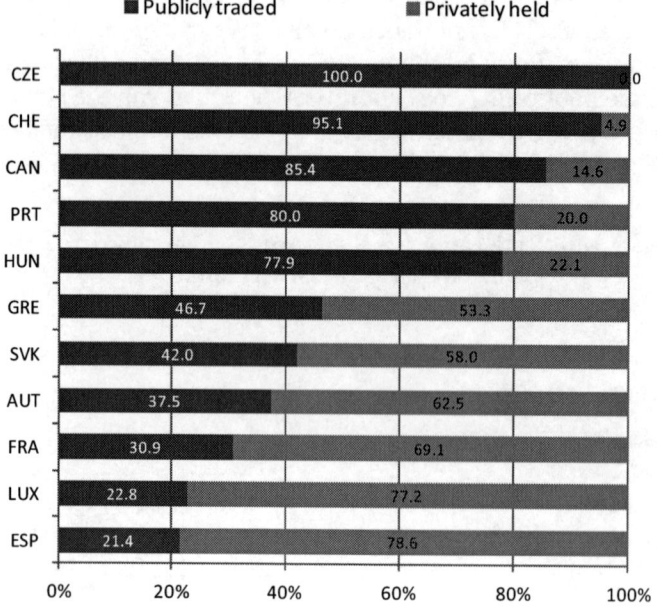

As a percentage of total equity investments

Note: Data refer to direct insurance only.
Source: OECD Insurance Statistics.

Fixed-income securities may also be an important source of vulnerability

In comparison with equity, fixed-income securities, which capture a large share of insurer portfolios, have been a source of vulnerability. The financial turmoil, by severely constraining the ability of corporations to access credit and liquidity, negatively affecting economic conditions, and thus increasing the probability of corporate defaults and increasing risk aversion, led to an extremely sharp widening of corporate spreads (see Figure 8). This widening required insurers to revalue a portion of their corporate bond holdings (specifically, those corporate bonds in their portfolios available for trading or sale – which are marked to market – as opposed to those held until maturity) to reflect lowered market values, and thus to recognise losses. The deteriorating environment for corporate bond valuations was partially offset, however, by a fall in risk-free interest rates – reflecting monetary easing – which is generally supportive of valuations of existing corporate bonds. In 2009, corporate spreads improved significantly, which may lead to gains in corporate bond holdings over 2009.

The credit exposures of life and non-life insurers to the banking sector through their fixed-income holdings of bank-issued money market and debt instruments has been a source of continued risk for the insurance sector, but this risk exposure has largely been mitigated by governmental measures to safeguard the safety of the financial system and the banking system in particular, as well as reduced by the improved financial position of the banking industry in 2009.

Figure 8. **Corporate bond spreads, 1995 – early 2010**

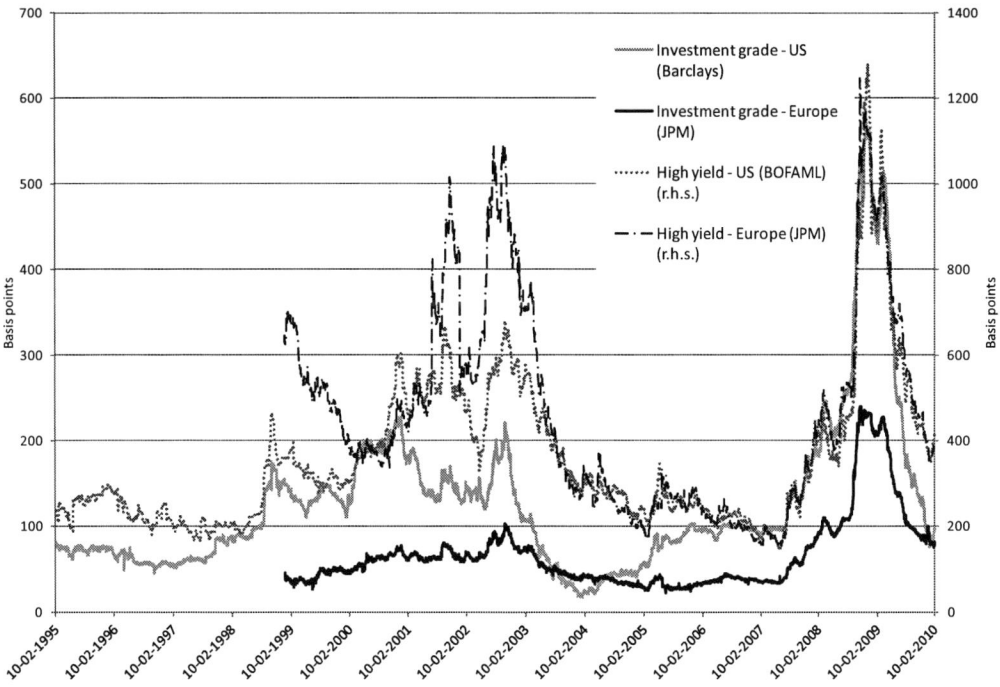

Note: Investment grade spreads are yield spreads over treasury benchmark bonds; high-yield spreads are spreads over investment grade bond yields.
Source: Thomson Reuters Financial Datastream.

Figure 9. **Share of public-sector and private-sector bonds for all segments11 in selected OECD countries, 2008**
As a percentage of total industry bond investment

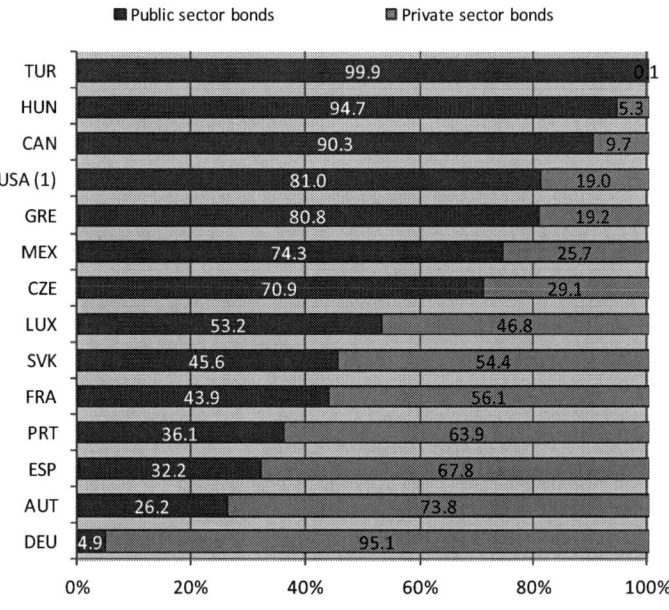

Note: (1) Data for US include both short-term bonds and long-term bonds.
Source: OECD Insurance Statistics.

The extent of insurer vulnerability to the widening of corporate spreads depends on the extent to which privately issued debt is held by insurers within their investment portfolios. In this context, it is relevant to note that within the "bond" category, the insurance industry in Canada, the Czech Republic, Greece, Hungary, Luxembourg, Mexico, Turkey and the United States, invest a significant share of the bond holdings in bonds issued by the public sector; by contrast, the insurance sector in Austria, France, Germany, Portugal, the Slovak Republic and Spain, display a greater preference for bonds issued by the private sector (see Figure 9).

Poor industry portfolio investment returns in some countries

There were only four countries (out of twelve for which information is available) with negative investment return reported in at least one of the segments. Based on this limited data, the picture is that the life and non-life segment experienced a degradation of investment returns in 2008 compared with 2007, with investment returns in the non-life sector showing greater overall stability relative to the life sector, where investment returns in some countries fell substantially in relation to 2007 performance, such as in Hungary, Belgium, Finland and the Netherlands (see Figure 10).

Challenging time for asset-liability management in the context of the crisis

Asset-liability management in the insurance sector has, in the context of the current crisis, been challenging. With the yield environment in the U.S. and Euro area reaching significant lows in late 2008 and early 2009 (see Figure 11), material risks arose on the liability side of insurer balance sheets, particularly for life insurers with interest-rate sensitive liabilities, such as deferred annuities or products with guaranteed yields. Lower government bond yields translate into lower discount rates used for the calculation of these liabilities, thereby increasing the present value of future payment obligations, and increasing reinvestment risk as insurers may find it more difficult in the future to secure fixed-income assets with sufficient yields to cover guaranteed rates. The impact of lower risk-free interest rates may vary from country to country, and from company to company, depending on the precise method used for the calculation of the discount rate. Where the discount rate used for the calculation of liabilities is derived from the yields on the fixed-income assets covering liabilities, and not independently extracted from government bond yields, there will be some offsetting effects on the asset side of the balance sheet.

In the United States the yield on the benchmark 10-year US government bond was 3.59% in end-January 2010, against 3.99% in July 2008 (See Figure 11). Since January 2009, the benchmark has displayed a rebound from its extremely low level in late 2008 and early 2009. This development has likely moderately eased strains on the balance sheets of life insurers with interest-sensitive liabilities.

Figure 10. **Average nominal net investment return by type of segment in selected OECD countries, in 2007 and 2008** (percentage)

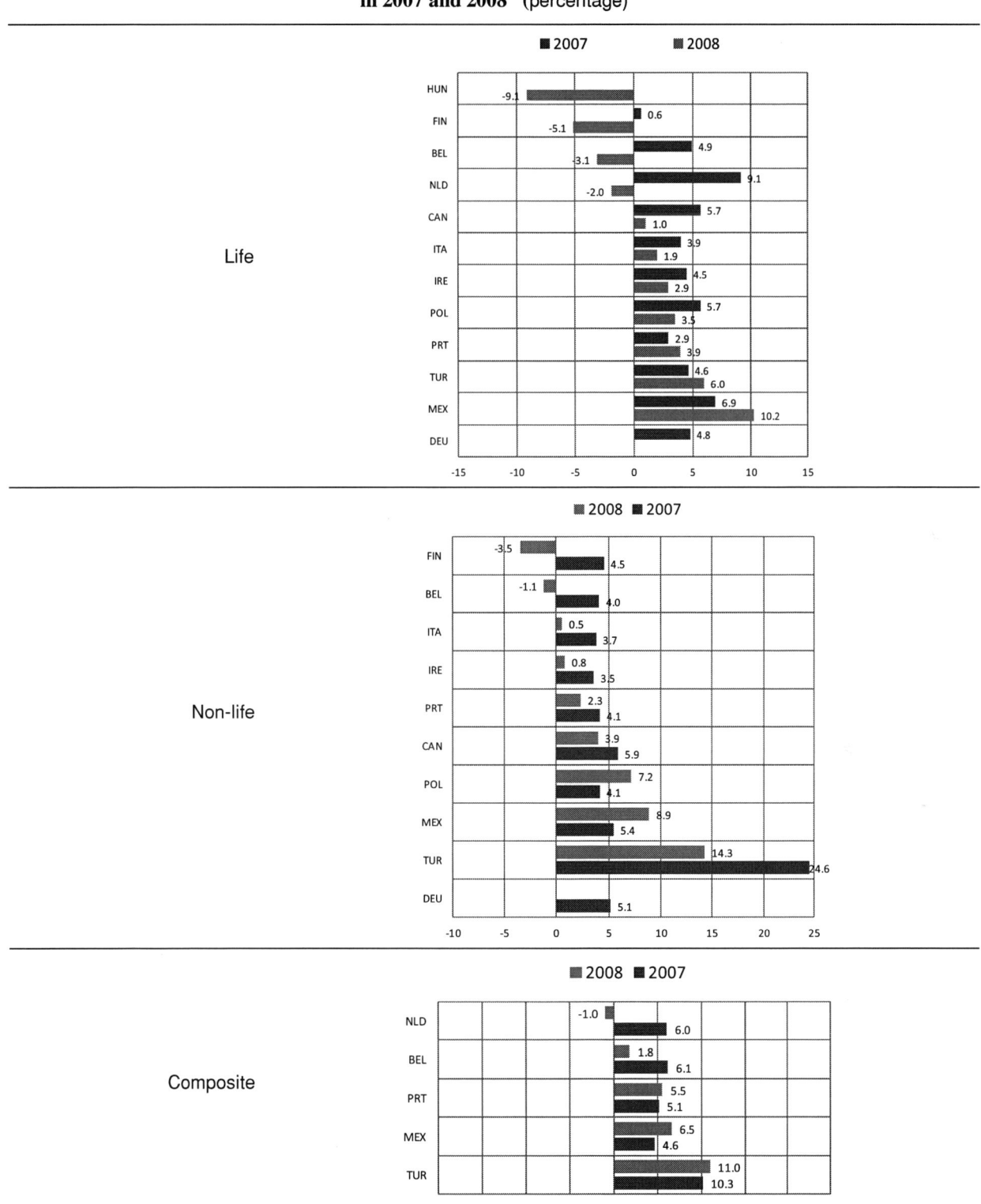

Source: OECD Insurance Statistics.

Figure 11. **10-year Government benchmark bond yields, Jan. 2004 – Jan. 2010**

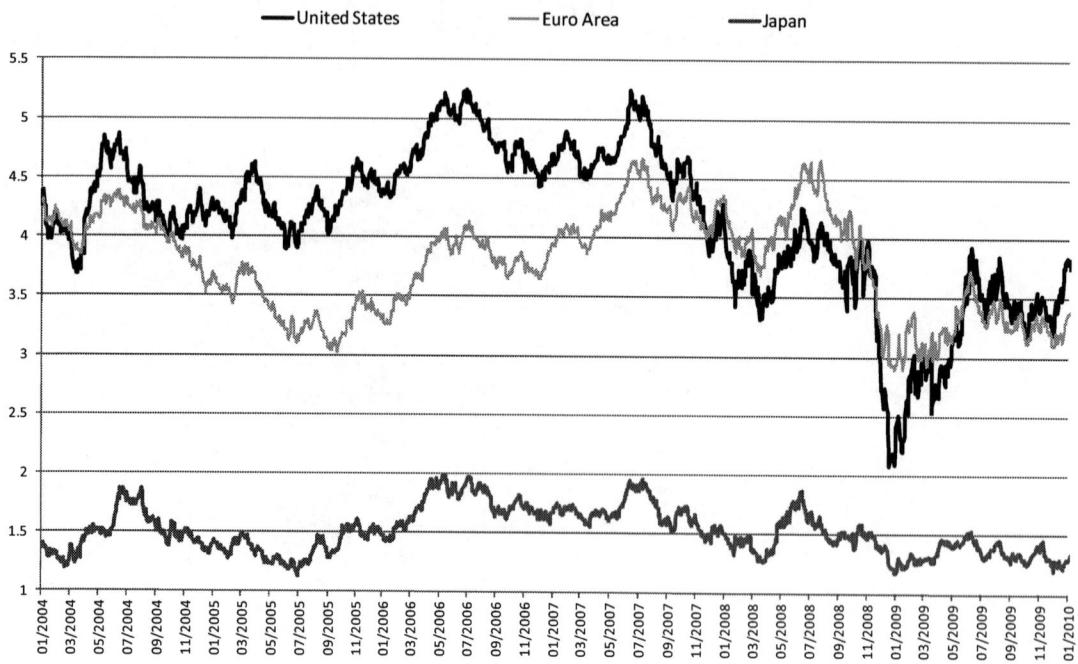

Source: Thomson Reuters Datastream.

In considering the balance sheets risks of life insurers, it is important to recognise that their balance sheets have, in recent years, grown substantially due to high growth rates in unit-linked insurance products, which are investment-type products similar to mutual funds, where the investment risk resides with the policy holder, not the insurer (see Figure 13 for the proportion of gross premiums in 2008, or for the latest year available, attributable to unit-linked products in selected OECD countries). To the extent that unit-linked products make up a large share of insurer assets, market, credit, and interest rate risks are borne by policy holders, not by the insurers. Life insurers that sold relatively risky products to customers with low risk tolerances may, as a result of the crisis, face increased reputational risk. The Madoff scandal has revealed that unit-linked products of some European insurers had invested directly or indirectly in Madoff funds.

Premiums

Despite the economic slowdown, many OECD countries still displayed robust growth of premiums in the life segment and steady growth in the non-life segment in 2008

For the reporting OECD countries, total aggregate net premiums written in the non-life sector increased on average by 5.1% in 2008 compared to 2007. In the life sector, premiums displayed slightly higher growth; the OECD-weighted average net premium increased by 6.2%. However, five countries, namely, Australia, Hungary, Ireland, Italy and Luxembourg, experienced a sharp drop in their life segment, respectively -11.7%, -9.0%, -14.9%, -12.8%, -18.2%.

Figure 12. **Growth in life and non-life insurance net premiums written in selected OECD countries**
2007-2008 (percentage)

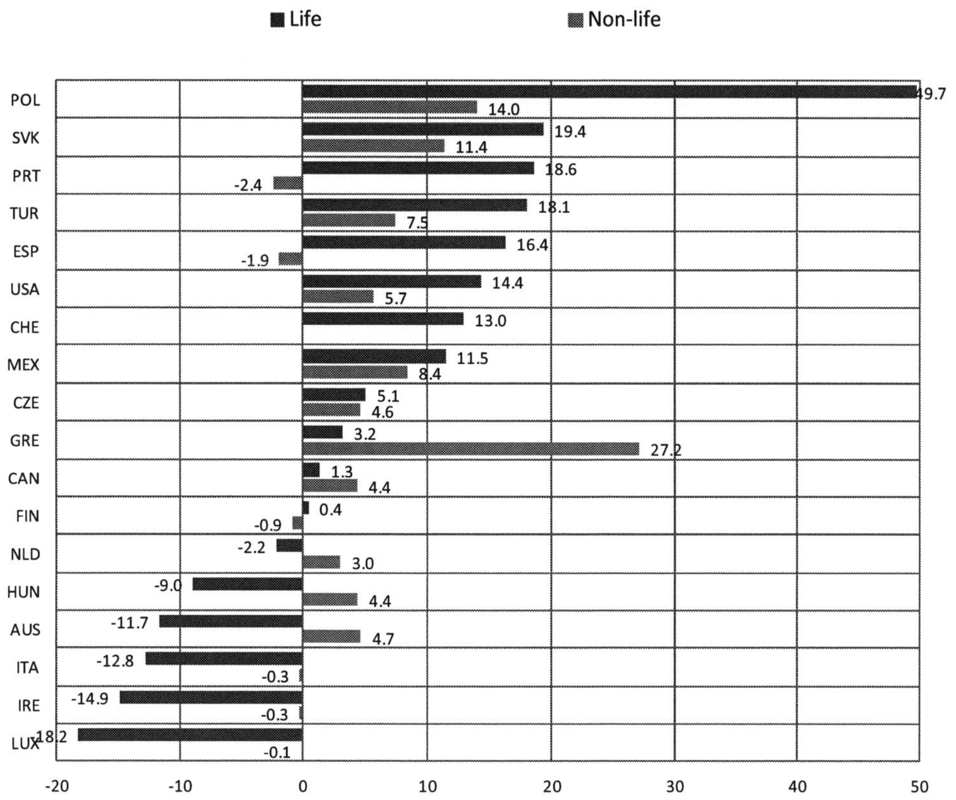

■ Life   ■ Non-life

Country	Life	Non-life
POL	14.0	49.7
SVK	11.4	19.4
PRT	-2.4	18.6
TUR	7.5	18.1
ESP	-1.9	16.4
USA	5.7	14.4
CHE		13.0
MEX	8.4	11.5
CZE	4.6	5.1
GRE	3.2	27.2
CAN	1.3	4.4
FIN	-0.9	0.4
NLD	-2.2	3.0
HUN	-9.0	4.4
AUS	-11.7	4.7
ITA	-12.8	-0.3
IRE	-14.9	-0.3
LUX	-18.2	-0.1

Source: OECD Insurance Statistics.

While detailed 2008 premium data is not yet available, information provided to date by member countries suggests that premium growth in unit-linked business – which has constituted an engine of premium growth and profitability for the life insurance sector in recent years – took the brunt of declines in premium growth in the life sector. With a few exceptions, it generally suffered across OECD countries due to adverse developments and volatility in equity markets. For instance, in France, it has been reported that premiums for unit-linked business fell by 42% in 2008, whereas premium growth for non-linked life insurance business remained stable; in Greece, the drop was reportedly 23%.

More generally, premium growth for life insurance products combining a savings component moderated in some countries in 2008 in light of financial market and economic conditions and heightened competition from bank products. Increased market volatility also contributed to declining sales for variable rate products as consumers shifted their focus to fixed annuities with stable returns. In some countries, the drop in sales of insurance products with a savings component was dramatic; for instance, in Finland, sales dropped by more than 40% in 2008. Moreover, in some countries (*e.g.*, Greece, France, Hungary and Poland), there was an increased trend of surrenders on life insurance policies, which may have reflected attempts to limit losses, liquidity strains facing policy holders, or investment reallocation.

Figure 13. **Total life insurance gross premiums by type of contracts in selected OECD countries, 2008**

Percentage of total life insurance

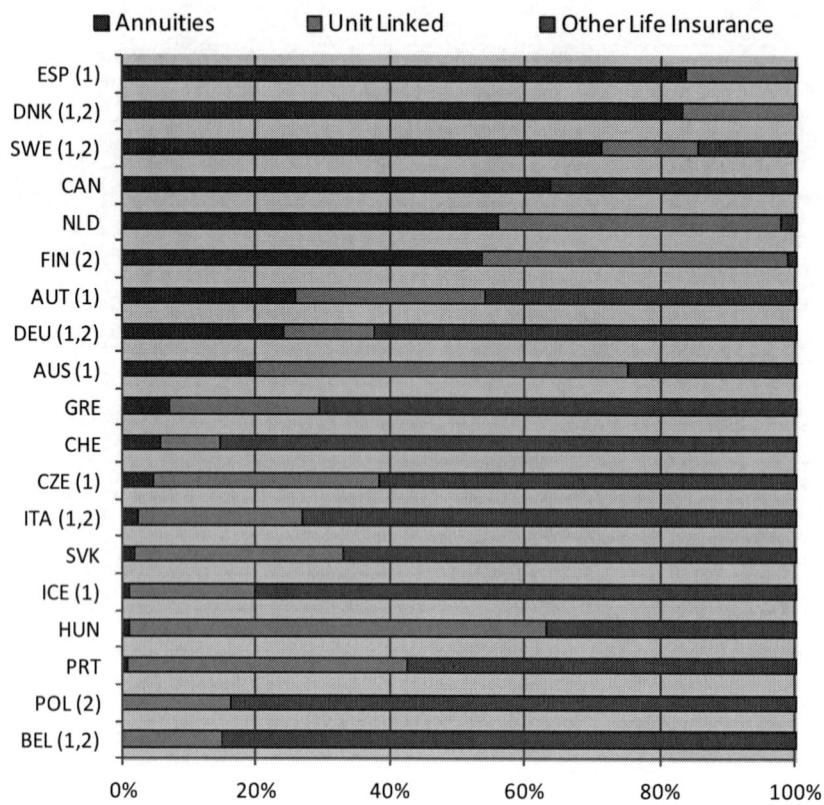

Note: (1) Data refers to the year 2007, (2) Direct business only.
Source: OECD Insurance Statistics.

Claims

Growth in claim payments between 2007-08 was highest in the life segment

On the basis of available data, a fairly sharp increase in gross claim payments, above 10%, occurred in the period in twelve OECD countries out of nineteen for which such information was available. Figure 14 shows four groups of countries. The first group consists of countries for which growth in total gross claim payments were steady in the range from 20% to 56%. This is the case of Austria, Belgium, Ireland, Luxembourg, Poland, Portugal, the Slovak Republic and Switzerland. The second group consists of Czech Republic, Finland, France, Greece, Mexico, Spain and Turkey that exhibited a moderate 2008 growth ranging from 9% to 15%. The third group, comprising Canada and the Netherlands, reported almost no growth or a slight decline in total gross claim premiums, respectively 1% and -3%. Finally, the fourth group consists of Australia and Germany that reported a sharp decrease in total gross claims, respectively -20 and -35%.

Figure 14. **Growth in total gross claim payments in selected OECD countries, 2007-2008**
(percentage)

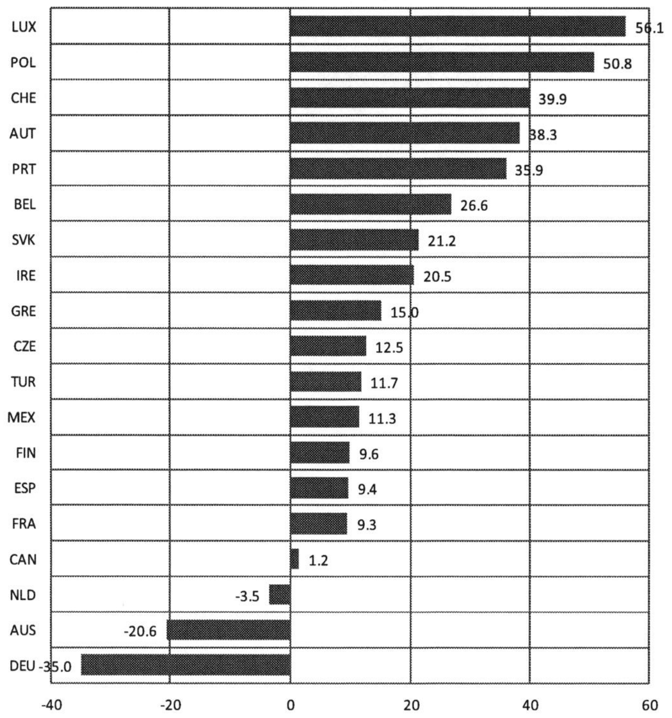

Country	%
LUX	56.1
POL	50.8
CHE	39.9
AUT	38.3
PRT	35.9
BEL	26.6
SVK	21.2
IRE	20.5
GRE	15.0
CZE	12.5
TUR	11.7
MEX	11.3
FIN	9.6
ESP	9.4
FRA	9.3
CAN	1.2
NLD	-3.5
AUS	-20.6
DEU	-35.0

Source: OECD Insurance Statistics.

Combined ratio

The underwriting combined ratio[12] measures core business profitability and allows the sources of profitability to be highlighted. An improvement in the combined ratio can be due to higher premiums, better cost control and/or more rigorous management of risks covered in insurance classes. Typically, a combined ratio of more than 100% represents an underwriting loss for the non-life insurer. A company with a combined ratio over 100% may nevertheless remain profitable due to investment earnings. An improved underwriting performance was observed only in Germany while in Austria, Canada and the Netherlands it remained stable (in the range +/- 5%). Ireland, Luxembourg and Switzerland experienced a substantial increase of their combined ratio (respectively, 33%, 44% and 139%).

In the non-life segment, the loss ratio[13] improved in Germany, and slightly in Australia and Canada (see Figure 16). Evidence suggests that while in Europe there have been no major catastrophes in 2008, a higher frequency of smaller weather-related events occurred, impacting negatively the loss ratios of major European insurance companies.

26 - IMPACT OF THE FINANCIAL TURMOIL

Figure 15. **Non-life combined ratio in selected OECD countries, 2007-2008**

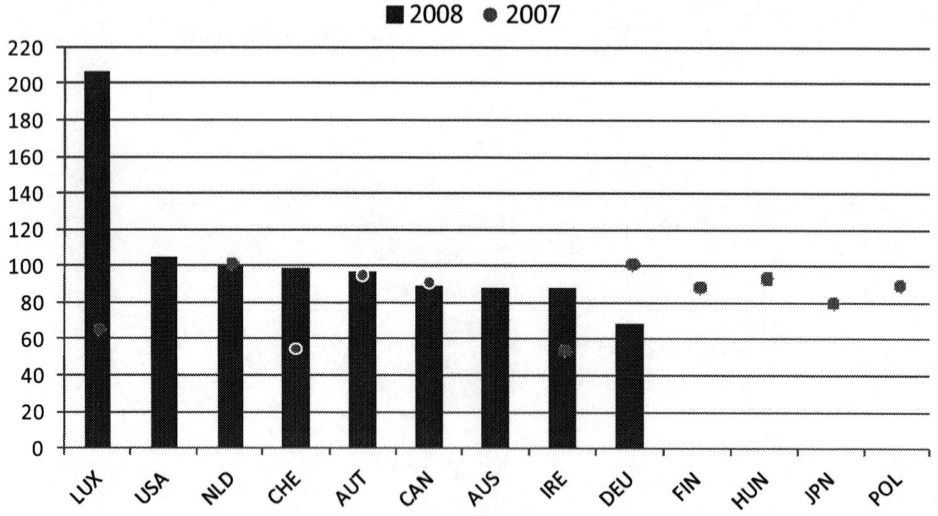

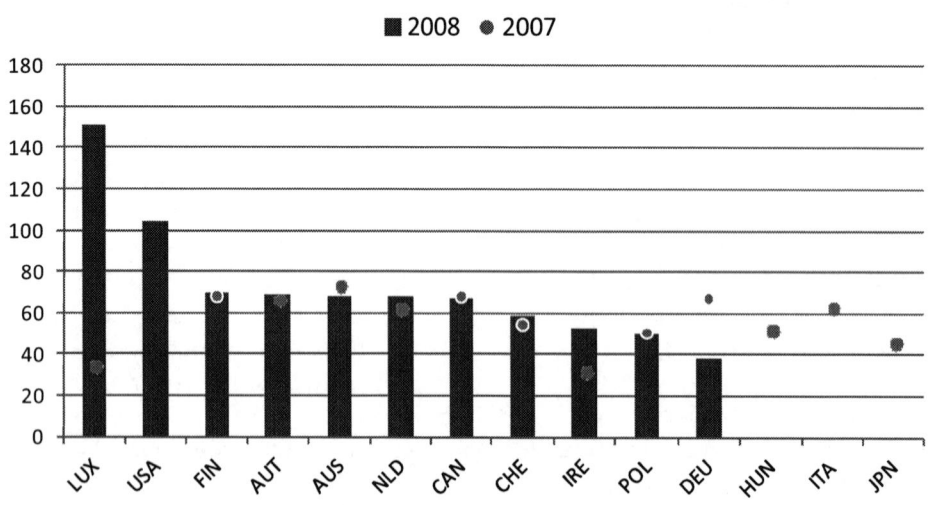

Source: OECD Insurance Statistics.

Figure 16. **Non-life loss ratio in selected OECD countries, 2007-2008**

Note: Given uncertainty regarding how countries have reallocated the business of the composite segment across the life and non-life segments and the need to ensure comparability across countries, the loss and combined ratios were not calculated for Belgium, Czech Republic, France, Greece, Mexico, Portugal, Slovak Republic, Spain and Turkey. [Note: The Secretariat is examining this issue to see if it can be resolved prior to publication].

Source: OECD Insurance Statistics.

Profitability

The profitability of the insurance sector was affected by the crisis in 2008

Industry profitability in 2008 in OECD countries (for which data is available) varied across countries and, within countries, across industry segments. Industry-level return on assets (ROA) and return on equity (ROE) have been used as indicators of profitability (at a company level, the former provides an indications of the return a company is generating on the firm's assets, and the latter an indication of the return a company is generating on its owners' investments). In a number of countries, industry ROA in 2008 was positive and, in some cases, relatively elevated, such as in France, Mexico, Poland and Turkey, However, in other countries, industry ROA fell below zero, for instance in Belgium, Finland, and the United States (see Figure 17). Similarly, industry-level ROE performance in a number of OECD countries was strong in 2008. However, there are a few country instances where ROE was significantly negative, such as in the life sector in Italy, Portugal and the United States, while Belgium recorded a sharp drop in all segments (see Figure 18).

Figure 17. **Return on assets (ROA) by type of segment in selected OECD countries, 2008**[1]

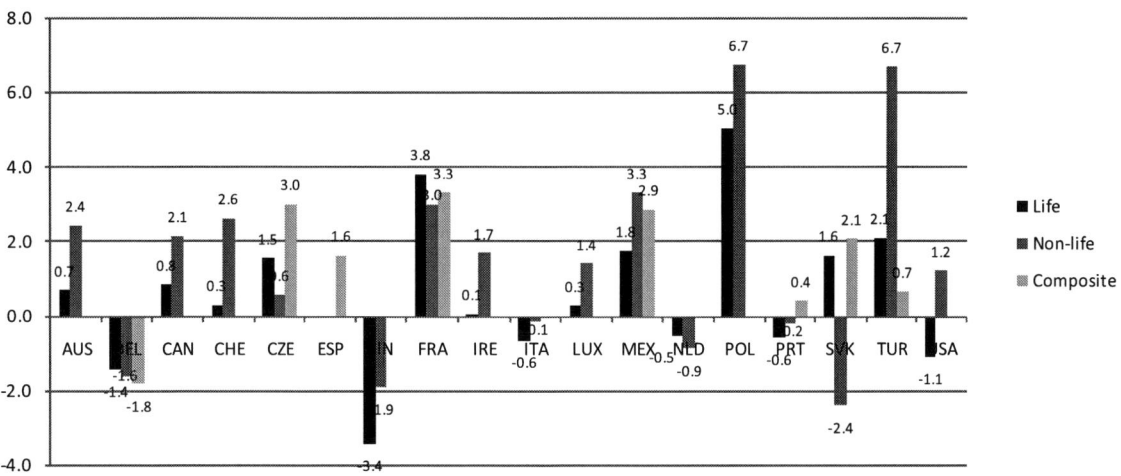

Note: (1) For the life segment, assets exclude unit-linked products. ROA was calculated by dividing segment net income for 2008 by average segment assets over 2007 and 2008.
Source: OECD Insurance Statistics.

As not all changes in a firm's balance sheet position flow into the income statement, but rather appear as changes in equity, it is helpful to examine changes in equity. This is particularly relevant for insurers since they hold held-to-maturity assets whose changes in value are not, under accounting standards, reflected in income until sale or impairment; instead, mark-to-market gains and losses flow directly into equity. Figure 19 provides a snapshot of changes in industry-wide equity levels from 2007 to 2008. In countries such as Belgium, France, and Portugal, the equity position across segments were severely impacted by the financial crisis, particularly in the life and composite sectors. Other countries, such as Italy, and the U.S., registered material declines, while, in other countries, such as Slovakia, the picture was more mixed. In a few countries, such as Luxembourg, Mexico, and Turkey, the life or non-life industries (or both such as in Turkey) recorded strong positive changes in equity.

28 - IMPACT OF THE FINANCIAL TURMOIL

Figure 18. **Return on equity (ROE) by type of segment in selected OECD countries, 2008**[1]

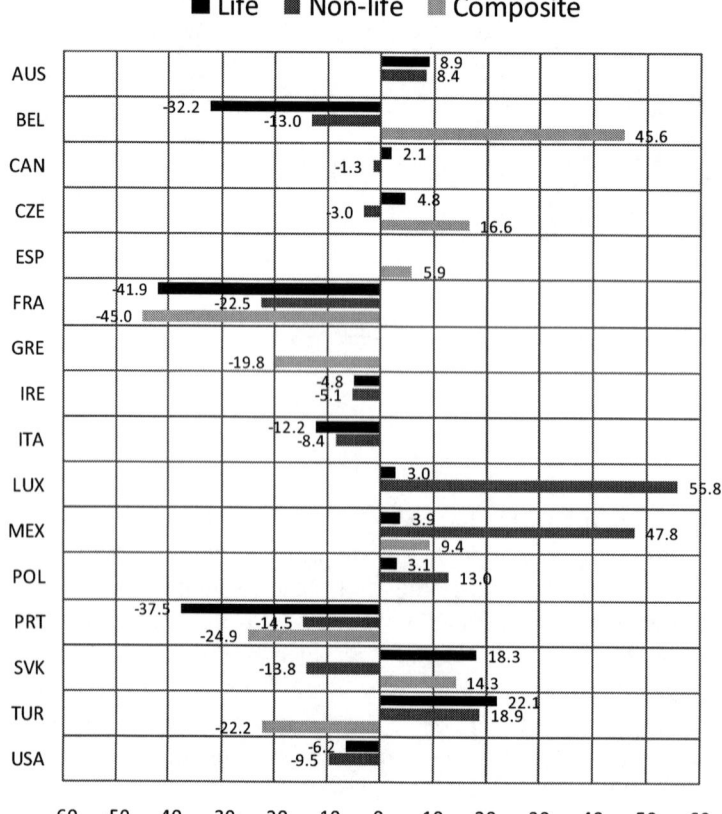

Note: (1) ROE was calculated by dividing segment net income for 2008 by average segment equity over 2007 and 2008.
Source: OECD Insurance Statistics.

Figure 19. **Change in equity position (2007-2008)**

Source: OECD Insurance Statistics.

Solvency

The crisis started having an important impact on industry solvency positions in 2008

The solvency margin, which puts available own resources in relation to the own resource requirement, shows that most countries, for which such information was available as of December 2008, still display solvency buffers over minimum statutory solvency requirements (see Table 2). However, there are countries in which the market turmoil and economic crisis had a significant impact on industry solvency position in 2008.

For instance, available solvency levels approached minimal levels in the life segment, for instance in Spain and, to a lesser extent, France, Italy, and Portugal. Table 1 (see earlier) shows the capital that has been raised by publicly traded insurers to replenish capital and raise solvency buffers. Given differences among countries (particularly outside the EU) in the calculation of solvency requirements, it is difficult to perform international comparisons of industry solvency levels.

Table 2. **Solvency margin**[14] **by type of segment in selected OECD and non-OECD countries**
2007-2008

Country	Life insurance 2007	Life insurance 2008	Non-life insurance 2007	Non-life insurance 2008	Composite undertakings 2007	Composite undertakings 2008
AUS	..	..	201.9	185.9	..	..
AUT	163.9	202.3	434.2	539.6	..	..
BEL	160.4	186.5	394.5	451.1	214.0	207.9
CAN	222.4	225.6	240.1	236.4	..	..
CHE	..	201.8	..	325.3	..	..
CZE	284.5	..	393.8	..	..	..
DEU	207.2	..	308.4	..	..	..
ESP	198.1	112.6	342.6	321.2	..	..
FIN	359.0	242.8	372.6	287.3	..	..
FRA	259.5	168.9	705.2	450.1	262.6	139.4
HUN	..	202.2	..	..	..	..
IRE	296.0	217.4	359.4	368.7	..	..
ITA	191.0	170.5	274.2	263.1	..	..
LUX	158.6	164.5	295.4	289.2	..	..
MEX	222.5	290.4	161.4	170.4	178.1	172.4
NLD	262.6	..	275.0	..	..	..
POL	347.3	285.8	667.0	642.7	..	..
PRT	148.4	139.6	221.0	200.0	165.4	154.3
SVK	247.2	363.8	672.6	608.0	270.3	311.6
TUR	295.6	309.4	140.0	148.0	366.4	351.0

Note: There are no composite undertakings in Denmark, Finland, Germany, Iceland, Japan, Korea, Poland, and the United States. In Turkey, composite companies are no longer permitted to operate; therefore, composite companies refer only to those non-life companies that still have outstanding life insurance policies in their portfolio.
Source: OECD Insurance Statistics.

Impact of the crisis on credit insurance markets

Dislocation and retrenchment

The financial crisis, and the economic crisis that has followed, has had an important impact on specific lines of non-life business, such as director and officer liability and professional liability, given the relationship between rising corporate insolvencies and ensuing litigation; these insolvency-related lines of business have reported large increases in premiums and some reduction in reinsurance capacity.[15] Possibly the greatest impact, however, has been on the availability of insurance used to facilitate commercial relationships, namely trade credit insurance (hereinafter called "credit insurance"). Credit insurance offers protection to firms supplying goods and services on credit against non-payment by their clients, due generally to client insolvency or default. Credit insurance has been referred to as the "life insurance" of companies: "Credit insurance…protects one of the key assets of the balance sheet, which is trade receivables".[16] This assertion is especially true as bank credit may depend on the existence of a credit insurance policy.

The implicit or explicit provision of credit by sellers to buyers is a common practice in OECD countries. For instance, in Spain, it is reported that 60% of GDP involved the extension of trade credit to buyers, with credit insurance coverage estimated to be 30% of the total volume of trade credit, or roughly EUR 200 billion.[17,18] In France, credit insurance covered, in 2008, roughly one quarter of company receivables in France, or approximately EUR 320 billion,[19] with a majority of risks covered by credit insurance linked to small and medium-sized companies. In the U.K., in 2008, credit insurers insured over £300 billion of turnover, covering over 14,000 UK clients in transactions with over 250,000 U.K. businesses. A private-sector credit insurer, Coface, has noted that for every 5 euros of short-term credit given to firms, 1 euro comes from banks while 4 euros come from suppliers.[20]

According to Marsh, total annual premium income for credit insurance in 2008 was over USD 8 billion, with 90% of business conducted by three major firms, Euler Hermes (36%), Atradius (31%), and Coface (20%).[21] In the past five years, the exposure levels of these credit insurers reportedly grew as they competed for market share through price competition that involved the assumption of increasingly marginal risks.[22] With the financial crisis introducing significantly worsened credit conditions in 2008 and early 2009, resulting in a rising number of payment defaults and corporate insolvencies, credit insurers started facing fast-rising claims, with loss ratios rising to 73% at Coface, 78% at Euler Hermes, and 99% at Atradius in 2008; these negative trends continued in early 2009 with Euler reporting an 88% loss ratio and Coface 116% in the first half of 2009.[23] In order to contain rising losses, the major credit insurers began reducing their exposures to specific countries, sectors, and buyers, leaving suppliers with either reduced levels of coverage or, in some cases, a full withdrawal of coverage[24]. Some industry sectors and countries reportedly became "off-cover" and loss-making policies experienced significant premium increases.[25] The sectors considered to be difficult to insure included construction, retail, commodities, electronic consumer goods, automobiles, and transport.[26] Moreover, multi-year credit insurance policies became difficult to find.[27] At the same time as coverage was being reduced, there was increased demand for credit insurance products given the desire of suppliers to control their risks in an increasingly turbulent economic and financial environment.

Concerns have been raised in a number of OECD countries about the "domino effect" of bankruptcies among suppliers caused by the reduction or withdrawal of credit insurance, threatening supply chains throughout the economy. Buyers slip into bankruptcy in the absence of trade credit; meanwhile, suppliers cut back on sales as a means of managing credit risks, further restricting trade credit and creating spillover problems, while other firms may still continue to do business and provide trade credit to high-risk buyers, but then potentially find themselves in bankruptcy as a result. Furthermore, some banks may be cutting back lending to small businesses with reduced or withdrawn coverage[28], thereby reinforcing the domino effect. Concerns about the domino effect led to calls for government intervention in credit insurance markets (particularly export credit insurance), which resulted, in some countries, in the creation of special temporary programs, mainly in support of export-oriented trade. For instance, the Confederation of British Industry called on the U.K. government or Bank of England to be the domestic credit "insurer of last resort" as a temporary measure.[29]

Interpretation of statistical data

Analysis based on balance sheet data has its limits, because shifts in risk exposure through the use of off-balance sheet instruments (*e.g.* interest rate swaps) or within the bond portfolio (*e.g.* towards longer-term bonds) may not be visible. Due to the lack of consistency in accounting standards followed across countries, some caution should be taken when interpreting the data. This complicates risk exposure assessments. Moreover, allocations to alternative investments are typically lumped together with "other investments". For such reasons, assessment that draws from official administrative data could be usefully supplemented by evidence from additional sources such as micro data from major insurance companies worldwide.

Table 3. **Asset valuation methodologies across countries**

Country	Valuation methods (as of May 2009)
Australia	Mark-To-Market
Austria	Book value
Belgium	Book value
Canada	Mark-To-Market
Czech Republic	Mark-To-Market
Finland	Mark-To-Market
France	n.d.
Greece	n.d.
Germany	n.d.
Hungary	Book value
Italy	Book value
Japan	Mark-To-Market
Mexico	n.d.
Netherlands	n.d.
Poland	n.d.
Portugal	Mark-To-Market
Russian Federation	n.d.
Slovak Republic	Book value
Spain	Book value
Turkey	Mark-To-Market
United States	n.d.

Conventional signs

n.a.: not applicable   n.d./..: not available

Notes

1. For further details on the role of monoline insurers in the financial crisis, see Sebastian Schich (2008), "Challenges Relating to Financial Guarantee Insurance", *Financial Market Trends* Vol. 2008/1, OECD, Paris.

2. See Sebastian Schich (2010), "Insurance Companies and the Financial Crisis", *Financial Market Trends* Vol. 2009/2, OECD, Paris.

3. See section on the *Impact of the crisis on credit insurance markets*, at end of Part A.

4. Financial data on pension undertakings operating solely in the retirement branch is excluded from all data on Turkish insurers.

5. In Turkey, composite companies are no longer permitted to operate; therefore, composite companies refer only to those non-life companies that still have outstanding life insurance policies in their portfolio.

6. Based on simple, unweighted averages.

7. Excluding assets linked to unit-linked products sold to policyholders.

8. Excluding assets linked to unit-linked products sold to policyholders.

9. Life, non-life and composite.

10. Excluding assets linked to unit-linked products sold to policyholders.

11. Life, non-life and composite.

12. Combined ratio = "Loss ratio" + "Expense ratio", where Expense ratio = (Gross operating expenses + commissions) / Gross earned premiums.

13. In order to be able to compare figures across countries, a simplified calculation of the loss ratio was used, as follows: gross claims paid as percentage of gross written premiums (the latter used as a proxy for gross earned premiums).

14. Solvency ratio (in %) = (available solvency capital / required solvency capital) x100. The purpose of the table is to highlight trends within a country, not across countries, given differences in solvency regulation.

15. See, for instance, *Casualty Specialty Update*, Guy Carpenter, September 2009, p. 5.

16. "What is trade credit insurance?", Adeline Teoh, *Dynamic Export*, 24 April 2009.

17. "Unas 45.000 empresas se beneficiarán de los avales de seguro de crédito del Consorcio de Compensación", Europa Press, 27 March 2009, from *www.lukor.com*

18. "Consorcio de Compensación de Seguros avalará operaciones de seguro de crédito, con un mínimo del 5%", Europa Press, 27 March 2009, from *www.lukor.com*.

19. See Communique de presse, "Dispositif de soutien et d'accompagnement à l'assurance crédit", 27 novembre 2008 (from *www.minefe.gouv.fr*)

20. *RiskAssur – hebdo*, 30 March 2009.

21. See *Trade Credit Insurance and the Global Credit Crisis* (Marsh, September 2009), p.1 (see global.marsh.com).

22. Ibid, p.1.

23. Ibid, p.1; Coface press release, "Coface continues to play its role, supporting companies despite the crisis", 4 September 2009 (see *www.coface.com*).

24. In Spain, for instance, in Spain, for instance, it is reported that 15% of Spanish firms lost their credit insurance coverage during the first 9 months of 2009 (see "El 15% de las empresas españolas perdió su seguro de Crédito", Inese, 30 October 2009, from *www.inese.es*).

25. Ibid, p. 2.

26. Ibid, p. 2.

27. See footnote 16.

28. "Credit insurance difficulties threaten banks' lending", *Insurance Daily*, 17 December 2008.

29. See CBI press release, "CBI calls for immediate government action to protect jobs", 24 November 2008 (see *www.cbi.org.uk*).

Governmental and Supervisory Responses to the Crisis in the Insurance Sector

Public authorities, at the outset of the crisis in mid-2007, focused on the liquidity positions of banking institutions given the remarkable and unprecedented seizure of international interbank lending markets in August 2007 and the sudden high risk aversion displayed by capital markets toward banking institutions due to concerns about bank exposures to sub-prime mortgage assets and the ability of some banks to manage their funding and liquidity risks. Central banks responded with the provision of large amounts of liquidity to the banking system.

By contrast, insurers, due to the nature of their assets and liabilities (in the life sector, there is a longer-term horizon and often charges associated with early surrenders of policies; and in the non-life sector, payment of liabilities is linked to the occurrence of an insured event), and ongoing premium earnings, were not subject to the immediate severe liquidity stresses affecting banks but nonetheless were affected by the broader shutdown in money markets. In addition, and more importantly, concerns were raised, given the high rate of growth of securitised markets and credit risk transfers in recent years, about the potential size of insurer exposures to sub-prime assets and derivative instruments referenced to such assets or exposures.

Governmental authorities and insurance supervisors therefore responded promptly to the crisis and began heightened monitoring of developments and sought to assess the size of insurer exposures to "toxic" and other sub-prime mortgage assets and derivative products linked to these assets. This intense monitoring has been ongoing since the outbreak of the crisis and constitutes one of the key elements of the governmental response to the crisis in the insurance sector. At the supervisory level, more frequent and detailed data have been collected from insurers, with a special focus on structured products such as collateralised debt obligations, asset-backed securities, and counterparty exposures; supervisory authorities have required insurers to conduct stress testing and scenario analysis; strong supervisory attention has been paid to the financial condition and risk management practices of insurers, particularly the large financial groups and conglomerates; there has been regular reporting to Treasury ministries; and special task forces have been established to facilitate coordination within and across governmental agencies.

In light of the stresses facing the banking system, and the desire to have arrangements in place to ensure that financial institutions buffeted by the crisis could continue to have access to necessary liquidity or capital as appropriate, governments throughout the OECD, in coordination with central bank authorities in some cases, have established special financial market stabilisation programmes. These programmes have typically addressed two key concerns: one, the issue of liquidity arising from market disruptions, through the provision of mechanisms for short-term financing, guarantees of debt issuance, or creation of special inter-institutional lending facilities, among others; and the second, the issue of solvency arising from exposures to toxic assets, through the establishment of authorities to provide equity injections or other forms of cash infusions such as the purchase of troubled assets. These arrangements are briefly discussed below in the context of the insurance sector, with a special and detailed focus on responses to the liquidity problems faced by American Insurance Group (AIG) given the significance of the near collapse of AIG Inc. and the policy and regulatory lessons to be learned.

Liquidity and short-term financing arrangements and the special case of AIG

For the most part, and most likely reflecting the differential liquidity stresses facing banks in comparison with insurers, programmes established outside of central bank lender-of-last-resort facilities to provide liquidity have largely targeted banks. Indeed, in a special survey conducted within the OECD Insurance and Private Pensions Committee (IPPC), only four in fifteen countries that had established special liquidity arrangements (out of a survey sample of twenty three OECD countries; see Table A.1 in Annex A) permitted access by insurers to these arrangements or created parallel arrangements for insurers. For instance, in Austria, under the new *Interbank Market Support Act*, insurers are eligible to join a liquidity "clearing house" and thus obtain access to inter-institutional market liquidity. In Canada, a Canadian Life Insurers Assurance Facility was created to guarantee the debt issuance of life insurance holding companies and life insurance companies regulated by the Office of the Superintendent of Financial Institutions; the guarantee provided by the federal government is subject to a limit of 20% of cashable liabilities in Canada. In the U.S., the FDIC Temporary Liquidity Guarantee Program, which guarantees senior secured debt issuance and deposits placed in transaction accounts at FDIC-insured deposit-taking institutions, permits the participation, on a case-by-case basis, and subject to regulatory approval, of approved affiliates of bank or thrift holding companies, which could in theory include insurers that own thrift holding companies.[1] The special liquidity arrangements established in OECD countries are generally expected to be temporary in nature.

While insurers, due to their business activities and risk profile, have generally not needed or been able to participate in the newly established special liquidity arrangements, the near-collapse of AIG Inc., viewed by some as the world's largest insurance group, highlighted the severe liquidity stresses that can beset large, non-bank financial groups, resolved in this case only by massive amounts of U.S. Federal Reserve emergency lending. The liquidity stresses at AIG had their origins in mounting losses in the derivative business (especially on CDS contracts written) carried out by AIG Financial Products Corporation and in the securities lending operations conducted through the AIG Global Investment Group (AIGGIP).[2] Both activities implicated the insurance subsidiaries of AIG: AIG's insurance subsidiaries had substantial derivatives exposures to AIG Financial Products (though, from the perspective of the U.S. life insurance subsidiaries, these exposures were not identified as material);[3] and AIG's U.S. insurance subsidiaries had, with the approval of state regulators,[4] pooled together their securities lending activities with AIG Global Securities Lending Corp. Initially, these off-balance sheet programs were not material in size and did not raise regulatory concern. However, U.S. insurance regulators noted a significant increase in the size of the securities lending program in an exam in early 2007. They also noted the duration mismatch, in that the non-insurance subsidiary running the program was now investing collateral proceeds from these investors in longer-dated mortgage, asset-backed, and collateralised debt;[5] collateral liabilities were secured by short-tenor notes, generally 30-days or less, issued to the securities borrowers, who shared in the proceeds of invested returns.[6] U.S. regulators worked with the U.S. life insurers to reduce the scope of this program from around USD 76 billion to USD 58 billion until the collapse of Lehman Brothers and others stopped the financial markets. Even then approximately 90% of the assets were performing. At this time, the potential AIG Holding Company downgrade was announced, and the impacts were felt by the U.S. insurers as well; counterparties began demanding their cash. U.S. insurance regulators had viable plans for using the liquidity in the U.S. life insurers to pay off counterparties of the securities lending programs and bring the collateral onto the balance sheet of the U.S. life insurers; though it may have involved regulatory action. Instead, the Federal Reserve worked out a plan to address the much larger derivative losses as well as the securities lending collateral call problem; initially, the U.S. life insurers were part of the asset sale plan to help AIG Holding Company repay the Federal Reserve.

AIG Inc.'s potential ratings downgrade sparked additional collateral calls by its CDS counterparties, many among the world's largest financial institutions. The perceived prospect of a systemic breakdown, in light of the collapse of Lehman Brothers a few days earlier and in the context of AIG's interconnectedness in global CDS markets, the broader market exposures to AIG (*e.g.*, bank and investment bank loans and lines of credit, money market mutual fund holdings of AIG commercial paper, dependence on AIG financial guarantees on the part of some policy holders, and considerable municipality holdings of AIG notes),[7] and broader economic considerations prompted the U.S. Federal Reserve, with the support of the Treasury, to provide a two-year credit facility of USD 85 billion to AIG on September 16, with an interest rate of 850 basis points above LIBOR on both drawn and undrawn funds. This revolving credit facility was granted under a special provision of the Federal Reserve Act that permits the Federal Reserve, in "unusual and exigent circumstances", to make loans to non-Reserve member institutions. The facility was pledged against the assets of AIG Inc., the holding company, and of its primary unregulated subsidiaries; these assets include AIG's ownership interests in substantially all of its regulated subsidiaries. The Treasury obtained preferred stock convertible into 79% of AIG's outstanding stock, which provided a mechanism to allow the government to benefit from any potential upside to the bailout.[8] AIG's Chief Executive Officer was replaced upon the establishment of the credit facility.

With AIG Inc.'s bankruptcy averted, but its future still uncertain, securities borrowers accelerated their return of securities to AIG's insurance subsidiaries, which placed large liquidity pressures on AIG and its securities lending collateral portfolio as AIG sought liquidity in order to avoid forced sales of the portfolio, which would have led to substantial losses. In order to contain this second wave of liquidity stress and avert further losses that more directly threatened AIG's insurance subsidiaries, the Federal Reserve, through the New York Reserve Bank (NYRB), stepped in again on October 6 and created a special credit facility ("Securities Borrowing Facility") that permitted the NYRB to lend to a number AIG domestic insurance subsidiaries up to USD 37.8 billion in order to allow them to return the cash collateral they had received from the securities borrowers. The facility relieved the pressure on AIG to liquidate its securities lending portfolio holdings, giving AIG additional time to dispose of these holdings in an orderly manner so that AIG losses and further market disruption could be minimised.

Furthermore, as an additional source of liquidity, four AIG affiliates, including AIG Financial Products Corporation, began participating in the Federal Reserve's Commercial Paper Funding Facility (CPFF) in late October, established under the same special provisions of the Federal Reserve Act that permitted the creation of the first credit facility for AIG. The CPFF involves the purchase by the Federal Reserve, through a special purpose vehicle, of unsecured and asset-backed commercial paper from eligible issuers.

Despite AIG's access to sizable central bank credit in September and October 2008, the Federal Reserve and the Treasury nevertheless agreed to further actions on November 10 in light of deteriorating credit and equity market conditions, which led to continued losses and liquidity pressures at AIG (particularly on its derivative contracts and its securities lending programme) and threatened a further ratings downgrade.[9] These actions involved a combination of new credit facilities and a capital injection. Specifically, the Reserve Board established a new lending facility that sought to bring a permanent solution to the problems at AIG's securities lending programme. Credit of USD 19.5 billion was extended under a new facility for the direct purchase of the assets of the securities lending portfolio from domestic AIG insurance subsidiaries and for their placement in a special purpose limited liability company (SPLLC). This sale involved repayment and termination of the Securities Borrowing Facility established on October 6. The Reserve Board also extended USD 24.3 billion in connection with the establishment of a separate SPLLC in order to bring the problem of outstanding CDS contracts to a close. AIG retained a first-loss exposure on both special purpose vehicles, respectively USD 1 and 5 billion.

The other component of the November 10 intervention involved a USD 40 billion capital investment in newly issued Senior Preferred Stock of AIG under the Troubled Asset Relief Program (TARP) authority that had been recently created. In combination with this investment by the U.S. Treasury, the Federal Reserve modified the terms of the original two-year credit facility by extending the maturity of loans to five years (due 2013), reducing the maximum amount available from USD 85 billion to USD 60 billion, and reducing interest rate and commitment fees. The facility was still collateralised by substantially all of AIG's assets, and the company continued to be required to apply proceeds of asset sales to permanently repay any outstanding balances under the facility.

Another set of measures by the Federal Reserve and the Treasury was announced in March 2009, involving a restructuring of AIG obligations to the Federal Reserve, continued AIG access to Federal Reserve credit, and the provision of access, under TARP, to an additional USD 30 billion of capital, bringing total equity support to USD 70 billion. These new measures were "designed to provide longer-term stability to AIG while at the same time facilitating divestiture of its assets and maximizing likelihood of repayment to the U.S. government."[10]. Overall, in 2008, AIG experienced roughly USD 99 billion in net losses.[11]

Capital levels and arrangements

In addition to addressing the liquidity problems raised by the market turmoil, governmental and supervisory authorities in OECD countries have focussed on the implications of the turmoil for the solvency position of financial institutions, including insurers, given their potential holdings of toxic assets and the possible impacts of adverse developments in equity and credit market conditions. Supervisory authorities have sought to adopt a pro-active approach, seeking to identify, assess, and anticipate actual and potential losses and, in some cases, taking actions to ensure that sufficient buffers are in place.

For instance, due to the extreme market turbulence, some authorities have taken action to ensure that capital was not unnecessarily depleted through dividends or the repurchase of shares. For example, in October 2008, the federal supervisory authority in Canada (OSFI) issued an advisory asking federally regulated banks and insurance companies to consult OSFI first before repurchasing their own shares, even where share repurchase programmes had been previously approved by OSFI. The rationale for the move was that "the current environment calls for increased conservatism in capital management". In Hungary, management letters were issued to insurers asking their management to initiate reviews of their dividend experiences. In the U.S., insurers are already required to submit a request for the distribution of dividends when the dividends are in excess of predefined thresholds, which ensure that capital is not imprudently depleted. In the context of some recapitalisation programmes (described below), such as in the Netherlands, insurers receiving capital infusions were subject to restrictions on dividend distributions. Overall, however, the majority of OECD countries that responded to the special survey indicated that no special actions had been taken in this area in light of market turbulence.

For insurers that have come under stress or for countries where conditions have been seen as difficult, supervisory authorities (or governments) in a few OECD countries have exercised some forbearance and exempted insurers from capital requirements or alternatively have varied requirements. For instance, in Finland, insurers serving the first pillar pension scheme have been temporarily exempted from requirements (but not those serving the second and third pillar schemes), whereas, in Iceland, insurers have been given longer deadlines to meet regulatory requirements. In Italy, a decree was issued that temporarily amended local GAAP requirements (for individual insurers only) to introduce counter-cyclical measures whereby book values of instruments could be used for valuations for 2008; moreover, the difference between book values and market values could be included in the calculation of the solvency margin, up to a pre-determined limit. In addition, measures have been introduced in some countries to lessen conservatism in solvency requirements. For instance, in the U.S., some life insurers have been permitted, by state regulators, to deviate from accepted accounting practices, with consequent effects on insurer capital; however, these measures are ad hoc and firm-specific in nature, and are required to be disclosed to the public by these firms in their notes to their financial statements. In the majority of OECD countries that participated in the special survey, no exemptions have been provided or at least have been publicly announced.

On the other hand, the financial crisis has been an occasion for authorities in some OECD countries to rethink prudential regulation and assess whether increased conservatism in solvency rules is warranted, including whether a counter-cyclical, or "over the cycle", approach to regulation should be adopted. In Canada, OSFI has assessed the capital framework in light of the crisis with a view to making it more risk-sensitive and ensuring that it is not pro-cyclical.[12] In Hungary, the supervisory authority has introduced prudential early warning requirements in order to monitor more strictly the capital and solvency position of insurers, *e.g.*, they have to meet a solvency margin of at least 120% and recognised but unrealised losses (*i.e.*, the difference between market value and book value of investments that are "available for sale" as defined by accounting standards) are now being continuously monitored. In Turkey, measures have been introduced to try to ensure that reinsurance arrangements are prudently managed. In the U.S., consideration has been given to whether solvency regulation for the insurance industry can be strengthened in light of lessons learned from the crisis, but no decisions have been made at this point. However, specific efforts are underway to strengthen the regulatory framework for financial guarantee insurers. In September 2008, the Insurance Department of the State of New York issued a letter outlining new standards to which the financial guarantee insurance business should adhere, which the Department will be seeking, for the most part, to formalise through regulations or legislation.[13]

In most countries, special programmes and legislation have been put in place to recapitalise financial institutions. As with the special liquidity arrangements, only a few OECD countries have included insurers as eligible participants in such programmes or under legislative authorities (see Table A.2 in Annex A). Among the 23 OECD countries that responded to the special survey, 13 countries have established special recapitalisation programmes or implemented legislative initiatives to provide for an authority to inject capital and, of these, only 5 countries have made provisions for insurers to be eligible for recapitalisation (or to provide insurer access to funding in an indirect fashion). In Austria, under the new *Financial Market Stability Act*, the Federal Minister of Finance is empowered to take measures – including the granting of loans, equity provision, and acquisition of shares – to recapitalise individual banks and insurance companies. In Canada, federal financial institution statutes were amended to grant the government the authority to inject capital into regulated financial institutions, including insurers. In the Netherlands, the government established, in October 2008, a EUR 20 billion special facility for the recapitalisation of solvent financial institutions facing unexpected external shocks. Under this facility, Aegon received EUR 3 billion in capital support. In Poland, legislation was established that would allow the Polish Minister of Finance to recapitalise certain financial institutions experiencing solvency difficulties. When institution regains its financial stability (*i.e.*, finds new investors), the Treasury could withdraw its further financial support. In the U.S., TARP was extended to insurers who have bank or thrift holding companies. Several large insurance groups applied for assistance and were approved. The special recapitalisation programmes for banks (and where relevant, insurers) typically have provisions requiring participants to be bound to certain terms and conditions, for instance in respect of corporate governance, dividend payouts, and remuneration. In a few countries, special ad hoc capital injections have been made into insurers outside of any established programmes: for instance, Ethias, the mutual insurer in Belgium (EUR 1.5 billion), and AIG in the U.S., as previously described.

Corporate governance, risk management, investments, and reporting and disclosure

In general, OECD countries already have legislative and regulatory provisions outlining requirements for sound corporate governance and risk management practices. That said, in some countries, some new measures were introduced in response to the financial crisis or consideration is being given to enhancing existing requirements (see Table A.3 in Annex A). Alternatively, some countries have increased their vigilance of corporate governance practices. For instance, in the Netherlands, the supervisor received more powers to take general measures. In Sweden, the supervisor has increased its supervisory activities; for instance, it is checking insurers' routine procedures regarding their register of assets, to which (policy holder) priority rights are attached. In Germany, a legislative proposal has been introduced into Parliament that would require members of the supervisory board of all insurance companies and of insurance holding companies to be liable to the same extent as executive directors and be sufficiently qualified to duly fulfil their supervisory functions. In the U.S., no specific actions are currently planned but there may be discussions, for instance, on the desirability of requiring insurers to conduct an "Own Risk Solvency Assessment" (ORSA), based on the Solvency II framework in the EU, in which insurers are required to determine their own solvency needs as part of the risk management framework.

Regarding investment rules, it appears, from the special survey, that many OECD countries have not sought to change insurer investment rules as a result of the crisis (see Table A.3 in Annex A). This finding is consistent with the observation noted earlier that insurers' exposures to toxic and other subprime mortgage-linked assets appear to be generally limited, though some insurers clearly have larger exposures to these assets. However, some countries have reported that they are amending rules or considering amending investment rules. For instance, in Austria, new limits for investments that do not have an investment-grade credit rating were incorporated into the regulations governing the assets covering technical provisions. In Finland, the investment rules governing insurers participating in first pillar schemes have been amended. In Germany, work is underway to make the investment guidelines for insurers more restrictive. In the U.S., consideration is being given to the need to modify state laws for investments that have caused problems in the crisis.

As noted at the outset, measures have been adopted by supervisors to increase the quantity, quality, comprehensiveness, and timeliness of regulatory reporting and disclosures, reflecting the speed and intensity of the financial crisis and the multiple and rapidly changing factors that can affect an insurer's solvency. These changes have mainly involved changes to reporting standards and the quantity or quality of disclosures, as opposed to any changes to accounting standards. In a few cases, such as Belgium and Italy, the change in reporting standards has affected solvency requirements or ratios. There was a range of views from those OECD countries reporting changes in reporting or disclosure requirements in the special survey as to whether these changes would be temporary in nature or permanent, though it is evident that many are likely to be temporary while others may be retained for the future. In the U.S., for instance, enhanced reporting of securities lending transactions will be a permanent change. Some countries have identified the need for further measures or improvements. For instance, Ireland noted the need to enhance the frequency of intra-group transactions reporting. In the U.S., consideration is currently being given as to whether more granularity should be obtained with respect to non-credit risks on a security-by-security basis.

Insurance groups and financial conglomerates

In light of difficulties faced by large financial conglomerates such as AIG, Fortis and ING, governmental and supervisory authorities have had to assess if there are any gaps in the current system of regulation and supervision of insurance groups and financial conglomerates, or if improvements could be made to the existing framework. A few countries have noted a few regulatory gaps (see Table A.4 in Annex A). For instance, Australia has noted that while new insurance group requirements were implemented earlier in 2009, work is underway on developing a broader regulatory framework that would cover requirements for all regulated financial groups; most recently, in March 2010, APRA released enhancements to the prudential framework for life insurance companies covering the operations of life company Non-Operating Holding Companies (NOHCs) in the areas of governance, fit and proper, audit and actuarial services, which will become effective in July 2010. Germany has noted that there is a gap in relation to the reporting of important risk concentrations at the insurance group level, which, in its view, should be done quarterly. In Turkey, recent regulatory changes have meant that the financial condition of major equity owners in insurance subsidiaries is explicitly considered as a basis for evaluating the financial condition of the insurance subsidiary. In the U.S., a regulatory working group has been established to consider possible changes to the NAIC Model Insurance Holding Company System Regulatory Act. A modern group supervision regime will be introduced in the European Union with the implementation of the new Solvency II directive.

In terms of measures initiated in respect to insurance groups or insurance-related groups, the most frequently identified crisis-related measures, based on OECD country responses to the special survey, were more extensive information-sharing and coordination activities among supervisors, and closer scrutiny of the activities of financial group entities. The former type of measure no doubt reflects the considerable international emphasis that has been placed on the establishment of new supervisory colleges. For instance, in light of the crisis, the Swiss Financial Supervisory Authority (FINMA) of Switzerland has reported that it has intensified contacts with other international supervisors that oversee other parts of those groups for which FINMA is primarily responsible. According to FINMA, enhanced information exchange regarding solvency, liquidity, risk management, and other key financial data have improved supervisors' awareness of possible areas of concern, and permitted faster and more proactive responses; in addition, more intensive contact has enhanced the examination of intra-group transactions, especially in a cross-border capacity. Some countries have noted continued impediments to cross-border cooperation, for instance, the lack of proper legal foundations for supervisory authorities to share information.

The de Larosière Group report on the future of European financial regulation and supervision, submitted to the European Commission in February 2009, highlighted the difficulties in proper cross-border supervision caused by a lack of cooperation, coordination, consistency and trust among supervisors and the existing gaps in preventing, managing, and resolving crises.[14] It proposed a number of structural measures to strengthen European coordination, such as proposals to introduce a legally binding mediation mechanism, operating through proposed new European supervisory authorities, to resolve disputes among supervisors regarding the supervision of a cross-border institution, that are still the subject of discussion. These measures were endorsed by the European Council of Ministers in March 2009 and have recently been advanced as legislative proposals. The legislative proposals would establish:

- A European Systemic Risk Board (ESRB) to monitor and assess risks to the stability of the financial system as a whole. The ESRB would provide early warning of systemic risks and, where necessary, recommend corrective actions.

- A European System of Financial Supervisors (ESFS) for the supervision of individual financial institutions, consisting of a network of national financial supervisors working in tandem with new European Supervisory Authorities, created by transforming existing Committees for the banking, securities, and insurance and occupational pensions sectors and adding new authorities.[15]

Enhanced coordination and cooperation have also taken place at the national level. For instance, in Poland, a Committee for Financial Stability was established by statute in October 2008, replacing a pre-existing memorandum of understanding. The Committee is chaired by the Ministry of Finance and includes the National Bank of Poland and the Polish Supervision Authority.

Policy holder protection schemes, restructuring and insolvency regimes

The failure of banking institutions and the near-failure of AIG Inc. have raised questions about policy holder protection schemes. Whereas there may an expectation on the part of retail policy holders that they are covered by compensation arrangements similar to the banking sector, providing for relatively prompt compensation following an insolvency, the reality is different. As revealed by the special survey, not all countries have policy holder protection schemes and, where they do exist, they may be very limited or often exist only for life insurance or general (property and casualty) insurance, and not both (see Table A.5 in Annex A). In 2008, Australia established a policy holder protection scheme for general insurance. In Japan, the government renewed its legal commitment to provide assistance to the Life Insurance Policy Holders Protection Corporation of Japan in the event that there is a shortage of funds. There are currently discussions within the EU on the desirability of establishing policy holder protection schemes across the EU and basic uniformity in terms of coverage levels and design.

In light of increases to the amount covered by deposit insurance schemes, some policy holder protection schemes, such as in Canada, have increased coverage levels. In some countries, governments temporarily extended their guarantee of deposits to policy holders, as in Belgium (for certain, narrowly defined insurance contracts) and Canada. In a communication on 4 March 2009,[16] the European Commission indicated that it sought to reinforce policy holder protection schemes in Europe, along with deposit insurance schemes and schemes in the securities sector. There is considerable controversy surrounding the desirability of establishing policy holder protection schemes, given concerns about moral hazard and the view that policy holder priority rights in insolvency, combined with strong regulation surrounding technical provisions and covering assets, provide adequate protection.

There has also been movement to strengthen the failure resolution framework for insurers and other financial institutions. For instance, in Poland, legislation is being considered that would establish new powers for the Minister of Finance to take over financial institutions (including insurers) having solvency or liquidity problems and playing an important role in the financial system. Among the powers available to the Minister would be an ability to acquire shares from the distressed institution on a compulsory basis, but at prevailing market valuations. These shares could be disposed of at a later date through a public bid or transferred to another state entity. The question of failure resolution of non-bank financial institutions has been raised as a policy issue in the U.S., including whether such a framework would have permitted a more orderly wind-down of AIG Inc. and reduced the need for a bailout. Some OECD countries already have rehabilitation or restructuring regimes for insurers that provide some control over how an insurance company is wound down and permit the taking of control and transfer of insurance policies, although it appears, based on limited information provided through the special survey, that the powers of authorities under such arrangements may not be as powerful or comprehensive as under the restructuring regimes applicable to deposit-taking institutions.

Credit insurance markets

A number of countries decided to intervene to address problems in the functioning of credit insurance markets, particularly export credit insurance. With mounting evidence of cutbacks in coverage or the withdrawal of coverage by private-sector credit insurers, governments in many OECD countries, in spite of pre-existing policies or restrictions preventing public-sector provision of credit insurance of "marketable risks" (*i.e.*, those risks capable of being underwritten by the private sector -- typically short term and, if export-related, covering purchasers in OECD and EU/EFTA countries), intervened to ensure, at a minimum, that those firms that had suffered cutbacks in coverage could restore their coverage to pre-existing levels (so-called "top-up" coverage). A limited number of governments also offered coverage for firms that had seen their coverage fully withdrawn or for those firms seeking coverage for the first time. Table A.7 in Annex A provides a summary of interventions in credit insurance markets.

The provision of top-up coverage has generally been introduced as a temporary measure (6 months to 1 year, with some programmes extending to 2-3 years) and has focussed on the supply of short-term export credit insurance for developed country markets, given pre-existing products or programmes for developing countries or existing programmes for insurance of medium to long-term receivables (both viewed as "non-marketable risks"). In almost all cases where intervention has taken place to support export credit insurance, reliance has been placed on private-sector credit insurers to supply or market the complementary top-up coverage, with the state-owned export agency, state-owned financial institution, or the government reinsuring the risk or in some other form providing backstop or indemnification arrangements. Those purchasing this insurance have generally been required to retain some risk (*e.g.*, 10%) as a means to align incentives, and, in some cases, coverage limits per firm have been imposed. Limits have generally been placed on the cumulative top-up coverage provided by the government.

In some countries (specifically Belgium, Canada, France, Spain, and the U.K.[17]), governments have provided top-up coverage for firms that have seen a reduction in their domestic credit insurance limits. These domestically oriented measures have reflected concerns about the breakdown of internal trade and possible contagion effects of cutbacks in credit insurance coverage (and related bankruptcies) in light of a heightened risk environment. As with export credit insurance, reliance has been placed on the private sector to offer and administer this top-up coverage, with the government or one of its state-owned entities responsible for reinsuring or guaranteeing the risk. In some cases, governments have used mechanisms in place for the financial management of large-scale catastrophes, such as state-owned reinsurers, to administer the top-up scheme.

In addition to top-up coverage, some governments have decided to offer, on a temporary basis, more generalised coverage to those firms that have seen their coverage fully withdrawn and those seeking coverage and unable to obtain it, be it for domestic credit insurance or export credit insurance. While many governments have limited their interventions to offering top-up coverage in order to leverage off the risk management decision-making of private-sector credit insurers and, in this manner, limit taxpayer exposure (*i.e.*, allowing private-sector credit insurers to determine the amount of top-up coverage), a few governments have expressed concern about generalised problems in credit insurance markets and the shutdown of credit insurance coverage in certain high-risk areas, such as real estate, construction, automobile, trucking, and retail, as well as about the possible contagion effects of suppliers using, in the absence of credit insurance, more drastic means to manage their counterparty risks (*e.g.*, payment upon delivery), which could contribute to liquidity problems at purchasing firms and possible insolvencies. These schemes offering general coverage have been designed with a view to balancing the objective of ensuring proper access to insurance while retaining some measure of risk control, independently set by governmental authorities, *e.g.*: purchasers of the insured party should not represent a high probability of default (for instance, in the

French CAP+ scheme, coverage is provided only if the expected default rate within the next year lies between 2 and 6%); insured parties should retain a portion of the risk (*e.g.*, 15-20%); and maximum coverage limits per counterparty.

The design features of the schemes established to support credit insurance markets and their broad similarities suggest a number of operating principles, namely:

- The scheme should be temporary in nature, and minimise disruption to, and competition with, private insurance markets;

- Insured parties should retain a portion of the risk to ensure an alignment of risk management objectives (i.e., transact only with purchasers that are commercially sound);

- Private-sector credit insurers should provide the primary interface with the insured parties to ensure relationship continuity and (in top-up schemes) play a role as risk managers;

- Reinsurance arrangements or other forms of backstop arrangements should be relied upon, using pre-existing structures as appropriate given the temporary nature of the schemes (e.g., state export guarantee agency, state-owned reinsurer, pre-existing consortium); and,

- An overall cap should be placed on overall government coverage, with possible individual credit limit caps on counterparties and/or coverage limits per insured party.

That said, these schemes have not escaped controversy. The high premiums charged for public coverage have attracted criticism in a number of countries, as have the credit limits on counterparties (if applicable) and extent of retroactivity (both seen as limited). In addition, criticism has been directed at the timing of the plans, which some stakeholders have considered to be "too little, too late". Top-up schemes have been criticised, in particular, for encouraging reductions in private sector coverage and for not addressing the needs of firms that have found their coverage fully withdrawn.

Notes

1. See FDIC rule at *http://www.fdic.gov/news/board/08BODtlgp.pdf*.

2. Most of the assets of AIGGIG were from affiliates within the AIG group, with the result that AIGGIG was reportedly one of the largest investors in the fixed-income asset class. AIGGIG also created synthetic CDOs specifically for the investment portfolios of companies within the AIG group, using collateral from within the group (see "Extending the hand of friendship", FT Mandate, October 2006).

3. See speech by Chairman Ben S. Bernanke before the Committee on Financial Services, U.S. House of Representatives, Washington, D.C., March 24, 2009.

4. Report made pursuant to Section 129 of the Emergency Economic Stabilization Act of 2008: Secured Credit Facility Authorized for American International Group on September 16, 2008, p. 1.

5. At 2007 year end, the securities lending collateral portfolio was composed of the following: mortgage-back securities, asset-backed securities, and collateralised debt obligations (65%); corporate debt securities (19%); and cash and short-term investments (16%). See AIG's Form 10-K, December 31, 2007, p. 108, at www.aigcorporate.com.

6. According to Bloomberg, some state officials had indicated that AIG invested more than half the collateral in debt securities that would, on average, pay off in 3 to 10 years. Since AIG loaned bonds from overnight to 60 days, AIG faced a liquidity squeeze if securities borrowers decided en masse to return AIG securities and demand their collateral. Almost 2/3 of the roughly USD 78 billion in cash collateral was invested in mortgage-backed securities. Traditionally, securities lending programmes reinvest cash collatereral in short-dated, safe asset such as Treasury bills and short-term corporate debt, though some securities lending programmes may undertake more aggressive collateral investment strategies to produce extra yield. See Bloomberg, "AIG to Absorb $5 billion Loss on Securities Lending", June 27, 2008, and Wall Street Journal, "An AIG Unit's Quest to Juice Profit Securities-Lending Business Made Risky Bets. They Backfired on Insurer", February 5, 2009.

7. See report by SIGTARP (Office of the Special Inspector General for the Troubled Asset Relief Program, *Factors Affecting Efforts to Limit Payments to AIG Counterparties* (SIGTARP Report 10-003, 17 November 2009), pp. 9-11 for further details on the concerns that were raised by senior Federal Reserve and Treasury officials regarding a possible AIG bankruptcy.

8. See Vice Chairman Donald L. Kohn, before the Committee on Banking, Housing, and Urban Affairs, U.S. Senate, Washington, D.C., March 5, 2009.

9. Losses on the residential mortgage-based securities portfolios in the securities lending program and credit default swap protection that AIG Financial Products had written on multi-sector CDOs accounted for roughly USD 19 billion of the USD 24.5 billion

10. in losses recorded in the third quarter of 2008. A further ratings downgrade would have caused termination events on AIG Financial Products' derivatives contracts. See reference in footnote 6 as well as the Report Pursuant to Section 129 of the Emergency Economic Stabilization Act of 2008: Restructuring of the Government's Financial Support to the American International Group, Inc. on November 10, 2008.

10. Vice Chairman of Federal Reserve Donald Kohn written testimony before the Senate's Committee on Banking, Housing and Urban Affairs on March 5, 2009. His statement included references to the investment losses of insurance subsidiaries and other factors affecting the financial performance of AIG, but these references were made within the context of the 2008 Q4 GAAP results. See:
    http://www.federalreserve.gov/newsevents/testimony/kohn20090305a.htm.

11. Ibid.

12. OSFI has also made changes to ensure insurers hold increased levels of capital as the dates for specific insurance obligation payments become more proximate.

13. See *http://www.ins.state.ny.us/circltr/2008/cl08_19.pdf.*

14. See *http://ec.europa.eu/internal_market/finances/docs/de_larosiere_report_en.pdf*

15. See Commission Press Release, "Commission adopts legislative proposals to strengthen financial supervision in Europe", 23 September 2009.

16. See "Communication for the Spring European Council: Driving European Recovery", 4 March 2009.

17. The U.K. "top-up" scheme expired at year end 2009.

Key Policy and Regulatory Issues in the Insurance Sector

The financial crisis and related governmental responses have served to identify a number of policy and regulatory issues. Some of these issues have been captured by the Financial Stability Board (FSB); however, additional issues require consideration. In identifying policy implications or issues for the insurance sector, consideration should be given to the fact that the business model for insurance companies is, despite convergence between the banking and insurance sectors, generally distinct from those of banks and that the insurance sector has, overall, fared the crisis relatively well considering the extreme systemic stress events that occurred in 2008. That said, the financial crisis has raised issues that are common across the financial sector. The key policy and regulatory issues of relevance to the insurance sector include:

Corporate governance and risk management: The resilience of insurers in the context of the current crisis may be attributable in part to improvements in governance and risk management practices in recent years; however, there is scope for further improvements. Some of the lessons of the crisis include:[1]

- *Strengthening the risk management framework*: Insurers, along with other financial institutions, should have a comprehensive, integrated risk management system and effective communication and reporting systems to properly identify, assess, control (as appropriate), and monitor risks. It is argued in a number of reports, including the de Larosière report, that this framework should be supported by an independent risk management function. It can be argued that boards should be involved in defining the proper risk appetite for an insurer and oversee the risk management framework.

- *Fit and proper board members*: The crisis has demonstrated the need for board members to have sufficient knowledge, expertise, and time to oversee and direct a financial institution properly, and effectively challenge management. This issue is particularly crucial in the insurance sector given the complexity of insurance products and markets.

- *Compensation*: The crisis has highlighted the role of remuneration in affecting incentives, and consequently behaviour. While the capital markets activities of insurers may be less extensive than in the banking sector, insurers should pay due attention to excessive risk-taking behaviour, as well as potentially misaligned incentives throughout the organisational structure, including at the level of sales agents.

- *Reliance on rating agencies*: Insurers should not rely solely on the ratings provided by rating agencies in their risk management and investment decisions but should perform their own due diligence.

Regulation of monoline (financial guarantee) insurers: Establishing an appropriately robust regulatory and supervisory framework for financial guarantee insurers is necessary to ensure a continued role for financial guarantee insurance in financial markets and minimise potential systemic risks. An issue in this context is whether consideration needs to be given to a structural separation of financial guarantee insurance business: one branch for financial market products, such as securitised and structured products; the other for municipal and other state debt. While diversification of financial guarantee business can bring strength to a financial guarantor, there may be an inappropriate cross-subsidisation of business, with the stable lines of financial guarantor insurance (*e.g.*, municipal debt) effectively underwriting much riskier business. For instance, questions have been raised as to whether financial guarantee insurance on derivative products alone is an inherently sustainable business model.

Incentives of third parties in relationships with policy holders and build-up of risks: Insurance provides protection to policy holders against risks. In so doing, the provision of insurance may, if the policy holder can affect his risk environment and is not subject to perfect monitoring by the insurer, lead to moral hazard; that is, the policy holder, in the knowledge that he or she will be compensated in the event that the insured event occurs, may be less proactive in managing risks, unless the insurer can impose measures to limit such moral hazard. However, as has been demonstrated by events in the financial guarantee insurer industry, as well as by recent developments in credit insurance markets, third parties with investment or commercial relationships with policy holders, and by extension with indirect exposures to the underlying risks facing the policy holder with whom they are dealing, may request and come to rely on the policy holder's insurance protection for their own efficiency and/or risk management reasons (*e.g.* investors in the case of complex asset-backed securities backed by financial guarantors, banks in the case of borrowers purchasing credit insurance), and paradoxically could prove to be less diligent in monitoring risks. On a collective level, such reliance could lead to a build-up of risks and lend itself to indiscriminate responses by these third parties when conditions deteriorate severely and insurance coverage is reduced or withdrawn, or loses its credibility.

Nature and scope of insurance supervision: Consideration may need to be given to whether supervisory mandates and roles need to be broadened to ensure that proper consideration is given, on an on-going basis, to system-wide and macro-prudential issues (and possibly also cross-border matters) and to matters that go beyond retail policy holder protection. For instance, the interaction of sophisticated players in financial and insurance markets may create market failures, such as systemic instabilities, as demonstrated by the financial guarantee market; in this context, there might be an important role for insurance regulators and supervisors to ensure, in close coordination with other relevant regulators and supervisors, that an adequately robust regulatory and supervisory system is, where necessary, brought to sophisticated insurance markets and its participants. In addition, movement to risk-based supervisory systems should be promoted in line with the tendency toward risk-based systems of solvency.

Insurance markets and macroeconomic linkages: Closer attention should be paid by policymakers, regulators, and supervisory authorities to the linkages between insurance markets and macroeconomic conditions; for instance, it has been argued that, in industries like trade credit insurance, ample liquidity and benign macroeconomic conditions led to weakened underwriting standards, and by consequence to the build-up of risks, which inevitably had to be sharply reversed in the context of adverse economic circumstances, harming policy holders and further amplifying macroeconomic shocks. Moreover, there may be broader economic spillover effects arising from the actions of insurers collectively seeking to manage risks. Thus, any "macroprudential" approach should not simply look at macroeconomic risks to insurers or the possible systemic consequences stemming from the collapse of insurers, but also focus on insurance markets themselves and properly assess interlinkages between insurance markets and macroeconomic conditions.

Group and conglomerate structures, contagion, and supervision: The crises at a number of large, globally active financial conglomerates since the onset of the financial crisis has raised a range of issues related to group and conglomerate structures, including:

- *Integration of functions across a group, contagion risk, and legal entity controls*: The near-collapse of AIG, Inc. has suggested that the centralised integration of functions within an insurance group, while providing for considerable efficiencies, may create risks for the legal entities that are a part of the group if such risks are not appropriately managed across the group, with adequate controls and oversight of such outsourced activities at the local entity level. In the case of AIG, the centralisation of securities lending activities created large liquidity risks for the group, making it exceedingly vulnerable to a ratings downgrade or any other event that indicated a weakened credit condition. There may have also been legal risks associated with the centralised pooling of securities lending operations in a separate subsidiary. These factors effectively created considerable contagion risks within AIG that would have otherwise not existed or been more manageable if such operations had continued only at the single entity level.

- *Integration of functions and group restructuring*: It has also been noted, in the context of a group restructuring during the crisis, that the centralisation of functions may make it more difficult to sell off subsidiaries, as such entities may not have the developed internal functions and controls to manage internal operations efficiently and effectively, given possible previous dependence on centralised functions and controls.

- *Combination of business activities and contagion risk*: The failure of financial conglomerates containing major banking institutions and insurers has raised the issue of contagion risk posed to insurers within financial conglomerates. Indeed, the problems affecting financial conglomerates have confirmed the view that combining different financial activities within a group, even if such activities are conducted out of separate legal entities, creates contagion risks. These risks can arise to due reputation risks, concentration risks, operational risks, and other possible risks.

- *Simplicity and transparency of structures*: The crisis has highlighted the problems created by complex and opaque group structures. Such opacity hinders the ability of supervisors and stakeholders to properly understand the risks facing an insurer, and greatly complicates the swift and orderly wind-down, or transfer, of an insurer.

- *Proper consolidated supervision and oversight of unregulated entities within a group, including at the holding company level*: The crisis has highlighted the need for proper regulation and oversight of unregulated entities within a financial group, particularly at the holding company if it is unregulated or weakly regulated. There should be effective cooperation and coordination among supervisors responsible for a financial group, and adequate supervision and oversight of the holding company. Without a view of holding company operations, it is difficult for supervisors to understand interrelations among the entities within a group, including intra-group transactions, and understand the risks of the group as a whole and of the entities within it.

- *Extent of diversification benefits*: The financial crisis has highlighted the limits of diversification benefits in group structures. This raises questions about the appropriate recognition (if any) of diversification in the determination of solvency requirements. The existence of possible economic diversification benefits does not mean that the prudential framework should necessarily recognise such possible benefits.

Scope of insurance markets and consistency and comprehensiveness in regulation and supervision: With financial liberalisation, deregulation, and innovation, insurance markets have become increasingly intertwined with capital markets and the broader financial system. Instruments with similar characteristics of "insurance" have, arguably, appeared in capital markets in the form of derivative instruments (*e.g.*, credit default swaps). Moreover, insurers are increasingly offering savings and investments products that are similar to products in banking and securities markets. For instance, unit-linked or variable annuity products have assumed a large role in the business activities of many life insurers. The convergence of industry sectors, combined with the growth of financial conglomerates have accentuated differences in regulation, for instance the lack of uniform global standard on solvency in the insurance sector; furthermore, they have highlighted the scope for regulatory arbitrage across sectors. This cross-penetration, increased sophistication, and convergence of financial and insurance markets raises questions of comprehensiveness and consistency in regulation at both a domestic and global level and points to increasing risks of gaps arising in regulatory and supervisory systems.

Competitive impact of government intervention measures: The introduction of special crisis-related government intervention measures to support the banking system has raised "level playing field" issues between banks and other financial institutions such as insurers. OECD countries have, in most cases, not included insurers as eligible participants in government programmes supporting liquidity and solvency. In theory, there may be sound policy grounds for offering certain types of assistance only to banks, particularly in relation to liquidity support. However, the experience of AIG demonstrates the liquidity problems that may exist in insurance groups involved in a broad range of financial market operations separate from, but sometimes related to (*e.g.*, securities lending), the business of insurance. There are also liquidity risks associated with the offering, by insurers, of banking-type insurance products. With respect to supporting the solvency position of financial institutions, questions can be raised as to whether it is appropriate to limit participation in recapitalisation programmes to banking institutions. The issue of a competitive level playing field, both domestically and internationally, should also be explicitly considered in governmental "exit strategies" from the crisis, and coordinated at the international level as appropriate.

Accounting standards: The use of mark-to-market accounting has been the subject of criticism, with some arguing that it contributed to the crisis and amplified it. However, ensuring proper transparency is important for investor decision-making and promoting market discipline. There is a need for a better understanding of the extent to which fair value accounting may have contributed to the financial crisis.

Financial education and literacy: The growth of unit-linked business, and attendant risks to policy holders, many of whom may have suffered from poor equity market performance, raises the question as to whether consumers have been appropriately informed of the risks of investing in these types of products and properly understand the options available to them within the product structures. Other new insurance products, which may have been fuelled by the credit boom (if not explicitly linked to the obtention of credit), such as payment protection insurance, may also present financial literacy issues.

"Too-big-to-fail" or "too connected to fail" problems: The bailout of AIG was unusual in that it was the first time that a financial conglomerate with significant insurance operations was considered to be "too big to fail". Typically, only large banks or banking groups have been considered in this light. While the original motivation for the rescue may have related to the complex financial activities being carried out through AIG Financial Products Corp., other considerations may have also been important, *e.g.*, the size and breadth of debt issuance (held by many financial entities including, importantly, money market mutual funds) and the role of the insurance subsidiaries in the U.S. and global economy. The fact that a financial conglomerate with significant insurance operations was deemed to be "too big to fail" raises challenging policy questions and raises the issue of how the systemic features or activities of such an institution can be properly reduced or controlled.[2]

Policy holder protection schemes: Well-designed systems of deposit insurance, with adequate levels of protection, are believed to have played an important role in maintaining consumer confidence in the banking system. While the insurance sector may not have the same liquidity challenges as banks, considerations of consumer confidence and protection may still arise and provide grounds for the establishment of a policy holder protection scheme. There is therefore the issue of whether policy holder protection schemes should be augmented (or where they do not exist, established). Consideration could be given by the OECD to cross-sectoral work in this area, involving a review and comparative analysis of compensation arrangements for banking, insurance, and private pensions.

Wind-up of large non-bank financial institutions: Since the near-collapse of AIG, Inc., increased attention has been turned to the question of whether there is a need for a special resolution and insolvency framework for non-bank financial institutions, including insurance companies. For instance, such a framework might allow, under specified circumstances, governmental authorities to take control of an insurer, issue loans and guarantees, acquire shares through compulsion, and restructure the company and its obligations and dispose of its assets as necessary in the public interest.

Notes

1. See also *IAIS-OECD Issues Paper on Corporate Governance* (July 2008).

2. For recent work on systemic risk and insurance, see *e.g.*: Mary A. Weiss (2010), *Systemic Risk and the U.S. Insurance Sector*, Center for Insurance Policy and Research, National Association of Insurance Commissioners; The Geneva Association Systemic Risk Working Group (2010), *Systemic Risk in Insurance: An Analysis of Insurance and Financial Stability*, Geneva Association; International Association of Insurance Supervisors (IAIS, 2009), *Systemic Risk and the Insurance Sector*, IAIS. Basel; and Scott E. Harrington (2009), *The Financial Crisis, Systemic Risk, and the Future of Insurance Regulation*, National Association of Mutual Insurance Companies.

Key Policy Conclusions from the Crisis

The OECD Insurance and Private Pensions Committee has, on several occasions, discussed the issues raised by the financial crisis and considers that it is important to draw some key policy conclusions from the crisis and its impact on the insurance sector in order to provide further impetus to financial sector reform. These policy conclusions are aimed at promoting financial stability, enhancing the protection of policy holders, and ensuring a level and competitive playing field. The conclusions are the following:

1. **Promote strengthened on-going surveillance of the insurance sector and cross-border supervision and information exchange**: The OECD insurance statistics framework will be enhanced and its surveillance efforts increased to the extent enabled by OECD resources. The International Association of Insurance Supervisors (IAIS) is also expected to enhance its surveillance activities. These efforts, as well as those of other international organisations and private-sector groups and associations, should be promoted to ensure a concerted and ongoing global surveillance effort on the insurance sector. Continued efforts should also be made to promote enhanced cross-border supervision and the exchange of information among relevant authorities in order to permit better monitoring and supervision of the insurance sector. The IAIS has made major strides in recent years to promote the exchange of information globally.

2. **Encourage greater consideration of macroeconomic linkages and macro-prudential risks in insurance sector policymaking, regulation and supervision:** Greater consideration should be given in policymaking, regulation, and supervision to the interlinkages between insurance markets and the broader economy, as well as to macro-prudential risks. While important, the risks facing individual insurers should be understood in a broader context, including in relation to other institutions in the financial system (particularly given differences in business models) and to broader macroeconomic conditions.

3. **Encourage convergence, over the long term, to a common core regulatory framework for internationally active insurers**: The financial crisis has highlighted the fragmentation of financial regulation and supervision globally and, thus, the possibilities for regulatory arbitrage and an unlevel playing field. While the insurance sector overall was not, unlike the banking sector, viewed as being seriously adversely affected by or as being a direct cause of the financial crisis, the insurance sector has nonetheless received scrutiny from financial sector policymakers, which has brought some attention to the fact that the insurance sector, unlike the banking sector with the Basel II capital adequacy framework for internationally active banks, has no common core regulatory framework for internationally active insurers. Given the importance of a level playing field and the benefits to be had from a more consistent and coordinated international approach, governmental authorities should work, as a long-term objective, to ensure a coordinated global regulatory framework for internationally active

insurers that would include certain common regulatory elements, including quantitative (*e.g.*, solvency capital), qualitative (*e.g.*, corporate governance, risk management), and disclosure requirements, as well as certain agreed methods of supervision and coordination. Efforts to be pursued by the IAIS to establish a common framework for the supervision of internationally active insurance groups, which will promote such convergence, should receive the full support of OECD member countries.[1]

4. **Ensure adequate and comprehensive regulation of group and conglomerate structures and eliminate gaps or differences among regulatory or supervisory systems where appropriate:** The crisis revealed important gaps in the regulatory oversight of large, complex financial conglomerates, including insurance-dominated groups. For instance, some insurance supervisors do not have the authority to oversee unregulated non-insurance entities that may control an insurer. Moreover, insufficient attention was paid to group contagion risks, for instance arising from the outsourcing of important operations to affiliates. The crisis also revealed gaps in regulatory frameworks more generally and the risks of differentiated approaches to regulation. Governmental authorities should work to ensure proper consistent and comprehensive regulation of insurance-related groups and conglomerates, and broad consistency of this regulation with the regulation of other financial sectors as appropriate. The IAIS initiative to establish a common framework for the supervision of international active insurance groups should provide a useful framework for starting to address some of these group and conglomerate issues. Moreover, the recent work of the Joint Forum on the differentiated nature and scope of financial regulation across sectors should be recognised and endorsed in this respect.[2]

5. **Strengthen insurer corporate governance standards**: The crisis has provided some direction as to how existing OECD guidelines on insurance corporate governance can be improved, for instance in relation to board practices and risk management. Taking into consideration recent work by the OECD Steering Group on Corporate Governance, the OECD is working to improve its 2005 guidelines on the governance of insurers and will seek to ensure global consistency with other relevant international principles and guidelines in 2010.

6. **Properly consider "too-big-to-fail" and systemically important insurers**: Financial institutions (whether engaged in banking, insurance, and securities markets) that are very large may be considered to be too large to fail, potentially leading to moral hazard and thus increased risk-taking behaviour. Governmental authorities should work to address this problem and mitigate risks and, in so far as it is present in the insurance sector, consider the specificities of insurers and their business model. Furthermore, attention should be paid to systemically important insurers which, while not necessarily large, may be so interconnected with other parts of the financial system that their failure could pose risks to financial stability or have an important impact on the broader economy.

7. **Ensure the orderly exit of failing insurers and ensure that governments have the full range of tools and powers to intervene effectively as necessary for the benefit of policy holders and the financial system overall:** Insurers should be allowed to fail in order to ensure competitive markets and preserve market discipline. The exit of failing insurers should be prompt and orderly. Governments should have the full range of early intervention tools necessary to

intervene, as necessary and appropriate, in insurance markets in a pro-active manner. Furthermore, in order to ensure efficient and orderly exit, an appropriate range of government resolution powers and procedures should be in place, including: (i) the authority to transfer business to other insurers; (ii) the authority to take control of an insurer; and (iii) the power to issue loans and guarantees, acquire shares (through compulsion if necessary), and restructure the insurer and its obligations and dispose of its assets as necessary. In this context, there should be work on promoting more internationally consistent and coordinated resolution and insolvency frameworks.[3] Moreover, policy holder guarantee schemes may be a useful complement to help protect consumers from the effects of insurer insolvencies. Under certain, exceptional circumstances, governments may wish to support a failing insurer. Tools should be available to governmental authorities to intervene quickly on an exceptional basis; these tools may include the provision of short-term liquidity, injection of capital, and provision of guarantees and reinsurance.

8. **Ensure adequate transparency in decision-making**: Governments should ensure that they work closely with the insurance industry in times of stressed environments as well as in normal times and that there is openness in discussions and transparency in decision-making. This open approach should help to ensure good lines of communication, ongoing monitoring of developments and risks, and constructive debate regarding appropriate policy responses.

9. **Promote financial education and literacy**: Governments should work to identify and address any financial education or literacy issues raised by the financial crisis, for instance in relation to unit-linked insurance products and other types of investment products offered by insurers. Such efforts should be incorporated into the country's broader financial education strategy.

Notes

1. See IAIS, "IAIS Approves Development of a Common Framework for the Supervision of Internationally Active Insurance Groups" (19 January 2010), at *www.iaisweb.org*.

2. Joint Forum (2010), *Review of the Differentiated Nature and Scope of Financial Regulation: Key Issues and Recommendations*, available at *www.bis.org*.

3. For recent recommendations on failure resolution frameworks for financial institutions, see the Basel Committee on Banking Supervision (2010), *Report and Recommendations of the Cross-border Bank Resolution Group*, Basel Committee on Banking Supervision, Basel (available at *www.bis.org*).

Annex A

Policy and Regulatory Responses to the Financial Crisis

Symbols
● = Yes ○ = Qualified answer (see comments) ✗ = No ☐ = Not available
The symbol ✗ is used to qualify a more general Yes (●) response or, in a few cases, to ensure clarity of responses. For those columns where no symbol has been inserted, assume a "No" response. This approach is taken to ensure a clearer presentation of responses.

Table A.1. **Liquidity or lending support**

	1.a Insurer eligibility to access central bank LLOR prior to the crisis	1.b Did any insurer access liquidity under these facilities?	1.c1 If yes, access has been provided only on a provisional basis	1.c2 If yes, access has been provided on a permanent basis	1.d Have any insurer received liquidity support?	2.a Government or central bank (non-LOLR) programmes established to facilitate financial institution access to liquidity / S-T lending	2.b Insurers as eligible participants?	2.c1 Direct provision of liquidity or loans by governmental or central bank? Authorities?	2.c2 Guarantees of commercial paper or bonds issued by insurers?	2.c3 Other special industry or government arrangements ?	2.d Have insurers obtained liquidity / loans through these arrangements?	2.e Are these arrangements expected to be permanent?	3. Special ad hoc liquidity or short/medium-term loans provided outside any established programme
Australia						●	×						
Austria						●	●						
Belgium													
Canada	○					●	●	×	●	×	×	×	
Czech Republic													
Finland						●	×	×	×	×		×	
Germany						●	●	●	●	×	×	×	
Greece													
Hungary													
Iceland						●	×	×	×	●			
Ireland						●	×	×	●	×			
Italy													
Japan													
Luxembourg						□							
Mexico						●	×					□	
Netherlands						●	×	×	×	×			
Portugal						●	×					×	
Slovak Republic						●	×	●	×	×		×	
Spain													
Sweden						●	×						
Switzerland						●	×	●		●			
Turkey						●	×						
USA	○	●	●		●	●	●	●	×	●	●	×	
Russia			●										

	Notes
1	**Canada**: Insurance companies are not eligible for LOLR facilities. However, in the event of a severe and unusual stress on a financial market or the financial system, the central bank can buy and sell from or to any entity (including insurance companies) any securities and any other financial instruments, to the extent determined necessary by the Governor of the Bank of Canada to provide liquidity. **USA**: If an insurer was part of bank holding company, the Federal Reserve Bank might have extended LOLR facilities to the Holding Company (similar to AIG). The information would be publicly available. **Russia**: This issue is under consideration.
2	**Canada**: Canada announced its voluntary and temporary programme, called the Canadian Life Insurers Assurance Facility (CLIAF), in its 2009 Economic Action Plan. More can be read on CLIAF at the following link: http://www.actionplan.gc.ca/initiatives/eng/index.asp?mode=7&initiativeID=32 . The CLIAF has since expired and was never formally drawn upon by insurers. **Czech Republic**: The "direct provision of liquidity or loans" has the form of newly established tool of the central bank called "liquidity-providing repo operations". Under this arrangement the central bank offered to provide liquidity to the banks and the Czech governmental bonds were used as collateral. This measure has not been used much by the commercial banks so far. **Hungary**: Relating to insurers. **Ireland**: Support is provided through a government guarantee of the liabilities of six credit institutions until September 2010. This guarantee does not apply to any insurer. **Switzerland**: In October 2008, the Swiss Confederation and the Swiss National Bank (SNB) undertook two coordinated measures to strengthen UBS's balance sheet that had been particularly affected by the crisis. On the one hand, the balance sheet of UBS was relieved of illiquid assets. In addition, the SNB concluded a basic agreement with UBS on long-term financing and on the orderly liquidation of illiquid securities and other assets to the value of up to USD 39.1 billion. As a result, UBS has been relieved of considerable risks in the form of other valuation adjustments. In order to limit the risks for the SNB, UBS created an entity funded with equity capital of USD 6 billion. Initially this will serve to cap losses. This transaction must be value adjusted creating a capital requirement for UBS which was set at CHF 6 billion. On the other hand, the Confederation strengthened UBS's capital base by subscribing to mandatory convertible notes to the amount of CHF 6 billion. In December 2008, another measure was introduced in order to strengthen depositor protection. The level of the protected deposits was increased from CHF 30000 to CHF 100000. A general revision of the depositor protection scheme will be launched in Q3 2009. **USA**: The utilization of TARP is still a moving target and has been used in various arrangements. **Russia**: Direct provision of liquidity or loans is under consideration.

Table A.2. Capital levels and injections

	4. Restricted dividend payments by insurers	5. Restricted share repurchases by insurers	6.a. Exempted insurers from K req'ts	6.b ↓ conservatism / K requirements	6.c ↑ conservatism / K requirements	7.a ↑ conservatism in provisioning / reserve requirements	7.b ↓ conservatism thereof	8. △ K / reserve req'ts for guarantees on unit-linked or variable annuities	9.a △ solvency requirements in future specifically in response to the crisis	9.b1 Life insurance	9.b2 General insurance	9.b3 Other insurance	10.a Programmes or initiatives to support capital position of financial institutions	10.b1 Insurers as eligible participants	10.b2 Use by insurers of these arrangements to obtain K?	10.b3 Are arrangements in placed expected to be permanent?	11. Special K injections provided outside of any programmes
Australia																	
Austria													●	●	×		
Belgium																	●
Canada		○				●	□	●					○	○		○	
Czech Rep.																	
Finland			●														
Germany													●	●	×	×	
Greece			●	●									●	×			
Hungary	○																
Iceland			●										●	×		●	
Ireland													●	×		×	
Italy		●	●										●	×		×	
Japan	●	●							●			●	●	×		×	
Luxembourg									□								
Mexico																	
Netherlands		○											●	●	●	×	
Portugal																	
Slovak Rep.													●	×		×	
Spain																	
Sweden						●							●	×		×	
Switzerland													●	×		×	
Turkey					●	●											
USA				●		●			●			●	●	●	●	×	●
Russia			●		●				●		●		●	×			

	Notes
4	**Hungary**: By issuing management letters we asked the management of the insurance companies to initiate the review of their dividend experiences. **USA**: Insurers are already required to submit a request to their state of domicile for dividends when they are in excess of predefined thresholds established in state law.
5	**Austria**: Some short selling restrictions. **Canada**: The Office of the Superintendent of Financial Institutions (OSFI) issued an Advisory in October 2008 on Normal course issuer bids. The Advisory states that all federally regulated financial institutions that have normal course issuers bids in place should first consult with OSFI before repurchasing shares. **Italy**: Repurchase of own shares is regulated by Italian Civil Code under Art. 2357, that has been recently amended by the decree-law no. 5 of 10 February 2008 (converted into Italian law no. 9 of 9 April 2009): in particular the maximum threshold of the own shares has been increased from 10% to 20% of the share capital, as an anti-(hostile) takeover measure. **Netherlands**: Insurers which received capital support have restrictions. **Portugal**: No Portuguese Insurance Undertaking is publicly traded in the stock markets. **Russia**: Russia has restrictions only for foreign investors.
6a	**Finland**: Yes, for 1st pillar statutory pension insurance companies does not concern 2nd and 3rd pillar schemes'. **Greece**: It has been proposed, as amendment to law, to postpone scheduled minimum guarantee level increase for 1 year. **Iceland**: They have been given longer deadline to meet the requirements. **Italy**: At the end of 2008 a law decree has been issued by the Italian government on accounting measures against the crisis (anti-crisis decree DL 185/2008). It was ratified by Law 2/2009 and endorsed for insurance sector by ISVAP Regulation n. 28 of 17th February 2009. It introduces temporary (1 year) counter-cyclical measures for financial statements drawn up with the local GAAP (only individual statements), such as, among others; the accounting rules which allow insurance companies to value held for trading financial instruments by using their half year-2008 book value (instead of the lower between average cost and realisable value according to market trend. Derivative financial instruments and permanent losses (*e.g.* Lehman Brothers) are not included in this option. The difference between such a value and the market value at 31 December 2008 is classified into a non-distributable reserve, part of which could be used both for improving the available solvency margin and covering technical provision under well specified limits: • *Solvency margin*: to a maximum threshold of 20% of required margin; this amount together with those of subordinated liabilities and preferred shares concurs also to the maximum limit of 50% of requested margin; • *Technical provisions*: the non-distributable reserve could combine to bring about no more than 2.5% of the Technical Provisions as a whole. Additionally, insurance undertakings which make use of this option, have to clearly identify further assets (included in the free assets), of at least the same value of the not written-down investments.

6b	**Greece**: It has been proposed, as amendment to law, the supervisory authority to be able to relax investment limitations. **Portugal**: In order to align the solvency regime with the accounting one, the use deferred tax reserves calculated according to the IAS 12 regime as a capital element was accepted. **USA**: Permitted practices have been extended by certain state insurance regulators under specific circumstances. These accounting deviations differ from insurer to insurer, but ultimately impact capital.
6c	**Hungary**: There were no legal changes but the Hungarian Financial Supervisory Authority introduced some prudential early warning requirements in order to monitor strictly the capital and solvency situation of the insurance institutions (*e.g.* they have to meet solvency requirements at least of 120%; furthermore we are continuously monitoring the unrealised loss (difference between market value and book value of the investments.) **Turkey**: Associated with the restrictions newly imposed on the amount of premiums to be ceded to the reinsurance companies a change in the "Regulation on Measuring and Evaluating the Capital Requirements of Insurance and Reinsurance and Retirement Companies" has made which entered into force on 1 March 2009. New risk coefficients are identified to be used in the case that the limitations related with the ceded premiums are exceeded. The aim of this amendment is to strengthen the solvency capital requirement in accordance with the increased risk in the reinsurance policy of the company. **USA**: Consideration is being given as to areas where insurance solvency regulation can be strengthened in response to "lessons learned from this crisis", but such decisions are being considered in the normal course of action. While some disclosure requirements for securities lending have been added, the more significant efforts (*e.g.*, group impacts, corporate governance) are being addressed through the Solvency Modernization Initiative.
7a	**Canada**: The crisis prompted the prudential regulator, Office of the Superintendent of Financial Institutions (OSFI), to review its capital requirements to assess if any changes where necessary to its rules. OSFI did not review the rules with a specific goal in mind in term of a quantitative impact (*e.g.*, making the capital test more or less conservative) but to make it more risk sensitive and to ensure that it is not pro-cyclical. OSFI has also made changes to ensure insurers hold increased levels of capital as the dates for specific insurance obligation payments become more proximate. **Turkey**: Being effective from 31.03.2008 companies are required to use chain ladder method for the calculation of provision for outstanding losses. Via this practice, companies were not allowed to make a provision for outstanding losses below the value found by the chain ladder method; therefore there was an increase in conservatism. On the other hand this regulation was not made especially on the light of the crisis; however, implicitly it can be considered as a form of protection from the possible negative effects of the crisis and an increase in prudence. **USA**: Consideration is being given as to areas where insurance solvency regulation can be strengthened in response to "lessons learned from this crisis", but such decisions are being considered in the normal course of action. While some disclosure requirements for securities lending have been added, the more significant efforts (*e.g.*, group impacts, corporate governance) are being addressed through the Solvency Modernization Initiative.
7b	**Sweden**: From the 11th of November 2008 the Swedish FSA changed its regulation for calculating the interest term structure for the insurance companies calculating their technical provisions. The modification of the regulation implies a possibility to involve even covered bonds in the calculation (before only an average of government bonds and swaps; now, as an alternative, the average of government bonds and covered bonds). The effect of this was that the interest term structure became a little bit higher which affected the technical provisions to be a little bit lower compared to the original regulation.

	USA: A project has been underway for a couple of years within the NAIC that contemplates moving away from the formulaic calculation of reserves for life insurers, and moves to a more principle-based method of such calculation. The end result of this will likely be a reduction in conservatism which is currently built into the formulas.
8	**Canada**: Changes were made to the capital requirements for segregated fund products to reduce volatility in capital requirements, to ensure that appropriate capital is held in respect of longer term payment obligations and shorter term payment obligations and to increase capital as payment dates become more proximate. (See revisions to MCCSR Guideline issued October 28, 2008). **Ireland**: Whilst there have been no changes to reserves or capital requirements in this regard, it should be noted that the Irish Financial Regulator operates a conservative regime, for example, by requiring insurers to hold 150% of the EU required solvency margin. **Mexico**: Capital requirements are currently established in the Insurance regulation. No new measures have been considered necessary given that current capital requirements have proven to be appropriate. **USA**: A project has been underway for a couple of years that contemplates possible changes to the accounting and reporting for separate account products (unit linked products). It's possible that these changes could result in some changes in the amount of funds carried in the general account for such guarantees, but it's too early to tell at this point. **Russia**: Unit-linked products are not allowed in Russia.
9a	**Germany**: Concerning the current German Solvency (I) System. Maybe changes to Solvency II. **Italy**: Even if solvency ratios decreased slightly this year, Italian solvency buffers remain adequate in both line of business; therefore no changes of the regime in force have been considered yet. **Mexico**: There is no specific policy chance due to the crises. However, authorities were working, even before the crisis, on a framework similar to Solvency II. **Netherlands**: The European Solvency II-directive is changed and also the implementing measures will be different. This will be in force in 2013. **Portugal**: Changes are expected to occur within the framework of the Solvency II regime. **Slovak Republic**: Solvency II proposed by European Commission takes into consideration also crisis situations. **Sweden**: Solvency 2 addresses this and negotiations are in progress. **Turkey**: Although not triggered specifically in light of the crisis, there are attempts for the adaptation of Solvency II to the Turkish insurance market. Risk-based capital which is one of the main arguments of the Solvency II shall be in effect after the completion of the required regulations and practices. In this framework, new solvency requirements are planned to be in force in the near future. **USA**: Consideration is being given as to areas where insurance solvency regulation can be strengthened in response to "lessons learned from this crisis", but such decisions are being considered in the normal course of action. While some disclosure requirements for securities lending have been added, the more significant efforts (*e.g.*, group impacts, corporate governance) are being addressed through the Solvency Modernization Initiative. In addition, the NAIC is currently considering accounting and reporting changes in response to the FASB crisis changes under FSPs issued for FAS 157 & FAS 115.

9b	**Netherlands**: A dampener approach for equity risk is introduced. Insurers receive more time to recover in times of stress. **Slovak Republic**: Mainly in equity risk. **USA**: In addition to the above areas of possible strengthening of financial regulation, the primary state regulators of mortgage insurers are considering adjustments to calculations for statutory Minimum Policy holder Position and Risk-to-Surplus Ratio.
10b	**Canada**: Although no specific programmes have been established to support the capital position of financial institutions, governing financial institution statutes were amended to grant the government the authority to inject capital into federally regulated financial institutions. **Hungary**: Relating to the insurers. **Ireland**: The Irish government has nationalised one bank and has injected redeemable preference share capital into two others. **Italy**: Anti-crisis decree (DL 185/2008) gave the possibility to the banks, in order to raise liquidity, to issue bonds (Tremonti bonds) that in turn are subscribed by IT Minister of Treasury. **USA**: TARP is extended to insurers that have bank holding companies. Several large insurance groups applied for the assistance and were approved, but few actually accepted funds.
11	**Belgium**: 1.5 billion (for one undertaking). **Hungary**: Relating to the insurers. **USA**: AIG.

Table A.3. **Corporate governance and risk management, investments, and reporting, disclosure and transparency**

	12. Introduction of corporate governance, risk mgt or internal controls measures	13. Introduction of measures on compensation practices	14. △ in regulation of investments	18. Issues raised regarding insurer transparency or reporting (including nature and frequency of data) to financial markets or to the supervisor	19.a △ financial reporting req'ts	19.b1 △ in accounting standards	19.b2 △ to regulatory reporting standards	19.b3 ← quality / quantity of disclosures	19.b4 Affect solvency req'ts or ratios	19.b5 Temporary changes only?
Australia	●	●								
Austria			●		●	×	●	●	×	×
Belgium				●	●	●	●	●	●	×
Canada				●	●	●	×			
Czech Rep.				●	●	×	●	●	×	●
Finland		●		○						
Germany	●			●						
Greece					●	×	●	●	×	
Hungary		●		●						
Iceland				●	●	×	●	●	×	
Ireland				●						
Italy			●	●	●	×	●	●	●	●
Japan	●			●	●	●	×			
Luxembourg										
Mexico										
Netherlands	●									
Portugal										
Slovak Rep.					●	×	×			
Spain			●		●	●	●	×	×	
Sweden	●				●		●	●		
Switzerland				●	●	×	●	●	×	●
Turkey				●	●	×	●	●	×	×
USA				●		×	●	●	×	×
Russia			●	●	●	×	●	●	×	

	Notes
12	**Australia**: APRA released, in November 2009, new prudential requirements on remuneration for authorised deposit-taking institutions (ADIs) and general and life insurance companies, which will become effective 1 April 2010. On 4 March 2010, APRA released enhancements to the prudential framework for life companies covering the operations of life company Non-Operating Holding Companies (NOHCs) in the areas of governance, fit and proper, audit and actuarial services. The standards have an effective date of 1 July 2010. **Germany**: See response to Q. 15. **Hungary**: No legal rule was introduced. **Italy**: ISVAP has already stated, irrespective to the crisis, rules related to corporate governance/risk management and/or internal controls which ask for an appropriate administrative and accounting organisation and an adequate system of internal controls/risk management, proportionate to the size and operational characteristics of the undertaking and the nature and intensity of company risks. Furthermore, these provisions envisage that the administrative body has the final responsibility over the system of internal controls and must ensure that it is always thorough, functional and effective, also with regard to outsourced activities. The administrative body ensures that the system of risk management allows the most significant risks to be identified, assessed and controlled, including those risks arising from non-compliance with regulations. Otherwise, strictly relates to the crisis, Regulation 28 places a big emphasis on the undertakings' corporate governance either when deciding to use the professed options or when evaluating the consistency of this decision with the future undertaking's commitments. In doing so they have to deliver complete and timely disclosure to ISVAP. **Mexico**: The following procedures, which existed prior to the crisis, are currently in place to assess the risk management practices of financial institutions and to promote sound risk management: - Identification, measurement, monitoring, limitation, control and spreading of the different types of financial risks that the insurance institutions face in their daily activity, according to international recommendations. - Insurance institutions must have a Risk Committee and an Internal Audit Department to establish the daily operations that imply risks and follow-up permanently on them. - Key notes have to be disclosed on the annual financial statements. This has the purpose of providing more transparency to the financial and statistical information of insurance companies. - A Corporate Surveillance System was implemented in order to allow the insurance institutions to send their corporate information to the regulatory authority. - There is work in progress to develop a Solvency II type framework, in line with the insurance principles proposed by the IAIS and the OECD. **Netherlands**: In general the supervisor received more powers to take general measures in light of the crisis. **Portugal**: The Portuguese Regulations on insurer's risk management and internal control already establishes requirements in line with the main lessons learned from the crisis. Nevertheless, it is worth mentioning that recently the ISP as issued a document containing a list of guidances in order to further reinforce the practical implementation of the said requirements. **Sweden**: The Swedish FSA has increased their supervision. For example we have checked the companies' routines concerning Register of assets with priority rights.

	Turkey: "Regulation on Internal Systems of Insurance and Reinsurance and Retirement Companies" which governs the principles concerning the internal control, internal auditing and risk management systems of insurance, reinsurance and retirement companies was published on 21 June 2008 in the Turkish Official Gazette No: 26913. However this regulation was not actually a response to the crisis, but instead was prepared on the basis of the article 4 of the Insurance Law No: 5684 and article 16 of the Individual Pension Savings and Investment System Law No: 4632 with the aim of continuously controlling and supervising the compliance of all works and transactions of the insurance and reinsurance company with primarily the laws, regulations, communiqués, tariffs and instructions, general terms and other legislation in effect as well as the internal circulars, management strategies and policies of the company and prevention and determination of errors, fraudulent and unlawful acts. **USA**: Nothing specific at this time, although regulators are beginning to value the idea of an ORSA (Own Risk Solvency Assessment) and it is likely discussions in this area will continue as a result of the NAICs Solvency Modernization Initiative (SMI) that began in the summer of 2008. A specific Working Group under the SMI Task Force has been formed to consider the development of a corporate governance framework. Some of the comments provided to this new group have been the result of new requirements for life insurers that are being drafted to add corporate governance requirements for principle-based reserving, but again this project has been underway for a couple of years.
13	**Australia**: APRA released, in November 2009, new prudential requirements on remuneration for authorised deposit-taking institutions (ADIs) and general and life insurance companies, which will become effective 1 April 2010 **Hungary**: No legal rule was introduced but the Hungarian regulation will be in compliance with the EU regulation if the new Commission Recommendations 2004/913/EC and 2005/162/EC as regards the regime for the remuneration of directors of listed companies and Commission Recommendation on remuneration policies in the financial services sector enters into force. **USA**: Insurers are already required to disclose in regulatory filings the highest paid officers and directors of the company.
14	**Austria**: Amendment of KAVO. **Finland**: Yes for 1st pillar schemes. **Germany**: Work in progress; investment guidelines for the insurers are supposed to be more restrictive. **Hungary**: Amendments to the legal rules are in progress. **Italy**: ISVAP Regulation N. 28, in transposing the modification in the reclassification criteria adopted by the IASB to the IAS 39, allows insurance undertakings (which drawn financial statements under the local GAAP) to assess, on a temporary basis (1 year), the financial instrument held for trading purposes at their 1H 2008 value, provided that: i) the valuation is coherent with the cash outflow of the undertaking; ii) the difference between such a value and the market value at 31 December 2008 is classified into a non-distributable reserve. **USA**: Consideration is being given as to areas where insurance solvency regulation can be strengthened in response to "lessons learned from this crisis", but such decisions are being considered in the normal course of action. While some disclosure requirements for securities lending have been added, the more significant efforts (*e.g.*, group impacts, corporate governance) are being addressed through the Solvency Modernization Initiative. It should be noted that one such possible area is investments, where a new NAIC working Group has been formed (Investment of Insurers Model Act Revision WG), which will consider the need to modify state laws for investments that have caused problems in this most recent economic environment.

| 18 | **Canada**: The financial crisis has impacted the nature and extent of ad hoc information requests. Where OSFI considered necessary for risk-based supervisory purposes, it has requested more detailed and/or more frequent financial information and disclosures from insurers on an individual entity or industry basis. OSFI is considering adjustments to regular reporting.

Finland: Discussion of timely disclosure in press.

Germany: A sample of the largest German insurers and IORPs (overall 32 companies, of which 26 are insurance groups and 6 single companies) must report on a weekly basis on their liquidity, the (group-) solvency margin, the assets covering technical provisions and any other risk that may influence the insurance group/entity. In addition ad hoc requests are carried out on a weekly basis and complement BaFin's regular reporting requests. Issues depend on current developments on the international financial markets, as well as insurance business related inquiries concerning, for example, the most covered combined ratios (more recent than in regular reporting), particular damaging events or qualitative assessments of 2008 concerning the level of damages. The specific impact of the financial crisis on the insurance cycle and the underwriting business is covered as well.

Hungary: The Hungarian Financial Supervisory Authority (HFSA) is continuously monitoring the impacts of the current financial crisis in the Hungarian financial sector. Since the 43rd week of 2008 in the framework of an extraordinary data submission the biggest 22 insurance companies are obliged to inform our Authority about the measure of the investment coverage of their insurance technical provisions and solvency capital. They have to send data on a monthly basis. These insurance companies comprise 80% of the total insurance industry investment portfolio, consequently nearly the full insurance sector is under the stressed supervision.

Taking into consideration that the crisis might expand, the Supervisory Authority started to measure the financial stability of the Hungarian insurance sector on the basis of stress test scenarios. This pilot stress test was based on deterministic with predefined parameters. Under the aegis of this project, the HFSA has established a stress test method. Its stress test focussed on undertakings with "strong" and "significant" impact on domestic financial system (these categories are based on HFSA's risk assessment system), and independent from other characteristics of insurance undertakings. The main purpose of the conducted stress test was to survey the robustness of domestic undertakings, individually. Stress scenarios primarily focussed on asset side developments and liquidity during the crisis with parameters that may faithfully reflect adverse future events. Further, the HFSA also required insurers selling unit-linked policies to assess the impact of an instantaneous increase in the surrender ratio (liquidation of assets, possible management tools, etc.). Due to the pilot nature of the project, no regulatory actions are planned on the basis of the conducted stress test. A public version of the output is available on the HFSA's web-site

Iceland: Questions have been raised regarding increased frequency of intra group transactions reporting.

Ireland: One of the largest Irish insurance companies was involved in an arrangement whereby its banking parent took a 7bn deposit from another bank and used it as collateral for advancing a loan of the same amount from the insurance company back to the other bank. This arrangement is alleged to have been used to bolster the perceived customer deposits of the other bank at its year end. The issue of transparency and reporting of this transaction and its legality are under investigation.

Italy: ISVAP has strengthened oversight activity by intensifying the communications the insurance undertakings are requested to deliver to the regulators: insurance companies have to send templates on investments, monthly (not quarterly as before), additionally life insurance undertakings have to send templates on premiums written and lapses/surrender on the same time frame. Some additional disclosure are requested related to those insurance undertakings which made use of the option included in ISVAP regulation 28 (*i.e.* the company must determine and send to ISVAP quarterly, instead of annually, the solvency ratio). |

	Mexico: Currently, not as a response to the crisis, the insurance companies have to disclose their key notes on annual financial statements, in order to provide more transparency to the financial and statistical information of the insurance market. **Portugal**: Regulations in place already contain an appropriate level of reporting and disclosure. Nevertheless there was an increase in the frequency of reporting of some elements. **Switzerland**: In 2009 FINMA introduced a new reporting tool which contains very detailed information about the investments and their risks. But the introduction of this tool has been planned years ago and is not a consequence of the crisis. On the other hand FINMA introduced a monthly ad hoc reporting to follow closely the influence of the financial crisis on the insurance companies focusing on the two key financial Data Solvency1 and the tied assets. **USA**: Many of the items that have caused problem are already well disclosed within insurer's annual statements (*e.g.*, directly held mortgage-backed securities and derivatives). However, regulators previously adopted additional risk charges for off balance sheet assets, adopted additional disclosure related to securities lending transactions, are clarifying when securities lending programs are off balance sheet, and are obtaining more granularity with respect to non-credit risks on an individual security by security basis.
19b	**Canada:** In response to the financial crisis, there have been several implemented and/or proposed changes to Canadian generally accepted accounting standards (GAAP) applicable to insurers over the past 6 - 9 months, these include: 1. In October 2008, amendments were made to Canadian GAAP that were similar to those issued by the IASB to conform IFRSs more closely with US GAAP with respect to the reclassification of financial assets out of the held-for-trading category into the available-for-sale or held-to-maturity categories in "rare circumstances". 2. In November 2008, there were proposed changes to Canadian GAAP, based upon the proposed improvements being made by the IASB to IFRS 7 that would require enhanced and consistent disclosures about liquidity risk and fair value measurements. 3. In April, the Canadian Accounting Standards Board decided to introduce changes, expected to be applicable by October 2009, to the Canadian financial instruments and impaired loan standards in response to the recent FASB staff positions adopted within the U.S. Note that OSFI does not have a comprehensive framework of regulatory reporting standards similar to the statutory accounting basis used by insurance regulators in the U.S. OSFI utilizes Canadian GAAP financial statements as the initial basis for regulatory capital determination, adjusting for a relatively small number of accounting valuations where considered necessary for solvency valuation objectives. As a result, changes in Canadian GAAP, or explicit changes to the capital rules, can impact solvency requirements or ratios. All regulated insurers must file with OSFI Canadian GAAP compliant specified quarterly and annual regulatory financial returns. OSFI has not fundamentally changed these returns in response to the financial crisis. However, OSFI is reviewing and changing certain aspects of the regulatory returns in response to the adoption of IFRS in Canada in 2011 and to address certain informational needs beginning in 2010. **Czech Republic**: There has been one change to financial reporting requirement for those insurers that use the Czech accounting standards (CAS). The change concerned bonds that are held to maturity issued within OECD whose credit rating is not lower than the rating of the Czech Republic and which cover technical provision excluding unit-linked business. Since January 2009, Czech insurers are obliged to value these bonds in amortised costs rather than fair value. This change only brings CAS to IFRS. As regards reporting to supervisor, the insurance undertakings were asked to report the data on their assets covering technical

provisions to the supervisor on a weekly basis (for a period of three months at the end of 2008). This was then changed to monthly periodicity and is still applied.

Italy: Temporary changes related to ISVAP regulation 28 (1 year) as above mentioned.

Netherlands: Supervisor had already the power to increase the frequency of supervisory reporting. Supervisory reporting standards where improved by the changes in legislation that came into force in 2007.

Slovak Republic: All insurer investments were reported weekly to National Bank of Slovakia.

Spain: The changes in our accountings standards have not been done because of the current financial crisis, but because of adapting our legislation to the IFRS.

Sweden: The larger insurance companies had to report their Top 30 of investments on a monthly basis (from the beginning every fortnight). This special reporting regime was temporary and is no longer required.

Switzerland: The solvency calculations have not changed but supplementary information to these systems have been introduced, *e.g.* stress testing with the solvency margin. The changes are temporary but we are reflecting about new requirements for the future.

Turkey: In order to monitor the impacts of the financial crisis on the insurance companies and to take measures as quick as possible, monthly and weekly reports which include important financial indicators are being collected from the companies. Based on the collected data, financial ratio and scenario analysis are made.

USA: Changes were made to disclosure requirements for credit derivatives and guarantees in accordance with U.S. GAAP. Updates to disclosure requirements for securities lending and related collateral were also implemented. Disclosure requirements for separate accounts as reflected in the general account have been updated. Accounting and disclosure requirements were adopted related to FAS 157 and fair value measurements. Other accounting and disclosure requirements related to impairment of loan-backed and structured securities were also updated. Accounting and additional disclosure requirements for securities lending transactions and other transfers of financial assets and liabilities related to FAS 166 and 167 are currently in development. Significant reporting changes were made for derivative instruments. Finally, RMBS accounting and capital requirements were based upon modelled results for expected losses compared to each insurer's carrying value of the RMBS rather than rating agency credit ratings of the RMBS.

Russia: Amendments to the law are planned.

Table A.4. **Insurance groups and financial conglomerates**

	15. Regulatory gaps identified	16. Improvements identified to existing regulatory system	17.a Regulatory or supervisory measures initiated	17.b1 Group-level solvency?	17.b2 Group-level liquidity mgt?	17.b3 Group-wide corporate governance and risk mgt?	17.b4 Closer scrutiny of activities?	17.b5 Information sharing among supervisors?	17.b6 Cooperation and coordination among supervisors?	17.b7 Other?
Australia	●									
Austria		●								
Belgium										
Canada										
Czech Rep.										
Finland										
Germany	●	●	●	×	×	●	●	●	●	
Greece										
Hungary										
Iceland			●	●	×	×	●	×	×	
Ireland										
Italy		●	●							
Japan			●	×	×	●	×	●	×	
Luxembourg										
Mexico										
Netherlands		□								
Portugal										
Slovak Rep.										
Spain										
Sweden			●	●	●	●	●	●	●	
Switzerland		●	●	●	●	●	●	●	●	
Turkey		●	●	×	×	×	●	●	●	
USA	●	●		×	×	×	●	●	●	
Russia										

	Notes
15	**Australia**: New insurance group requirements were implemented earlier in 2009 – APRA is currently working on a broader regulatory framework which would cover requirements for all prudentially regulated financial groups (including unregulated entities in those groups). A discussion paper is expected to be released on these proposals. On 4 March 2010, APRA released enhancements to the prudential framework for life companies covering the operations of life company Non-Operating Holding Companies (NOHCs) in the areas of governance, fit and proper, audit and actuarial services. The standards have an effective date of 1 July 2010. **Germany**: (i) Important risk concentration on insurance group level should be reported quarterly. (ii) Members of the supervisory board of all insurance companies and of insurance holding companies must be reliable to the same extent as executive directors and must be qualified enough to duly fulfil their supervisory functions (cf. also question 12). **Netherlands**: Of course Solvency II will improve insurance group supervision. However there are no further gaps identified. **Switzerland**: Regulatory gaps in a domestic sense no; however indirectly the ability to share confidential information in a meaningful way on a cross border basis with other supervisors where no, or a limited, legal foundation to do so exists still remains somewhat of a hindrance to our approach to effective global supervision. **USA**: Credit default swaps conducted by legal entities within a Group are not regulated and the NAIC has indicated that if no federal holistic approach is taken to better regulate this product, they will force any companies who sell such products that meet the definition of insurance to be regulated as financial guaranty insurers, with all of the capital and reserve requirements that such companies are required to maintain.
16	**Australia**: APRA had already done the work referred to in the answer to question 15 prior to the crisis occurring. The crisis has not indicated any additional elements to be considered/ further developed. **Austria**: Amendment of KAVO. **Germany**: The caveats addressed in no. 15 are part of a proposition of the government to the parliament to decide to amend the German Insurance Supervisory Act. Parts of the proposal (*i.e.* new governance requirements) are matters of intense parliamentary discussion. The outcome cannot be predicted at the moment (cf. also question 23 et seq.). **Italy**: One of the improvements that has been identified is the necessity to strengthen the cooperation and the exchange of information among supervisors involved in the supervision of cross border groups, both EEA and third country based. **Netherlands**: Currently still under discussion. **Switzerland**: In light of the recent financial market crisis, the Swiss Financial Supervisory Authority (FINMA) has intensified its contact with other international supervisors that oversee other parts of the groups which are supervised. Further information exchange in regards to the solvency, liquidity, risk management and other key financial data have also improved supervisors awareness of possible areas of concern and thus can be acted upon in a faster and more proactive manner. More intensive contact has also further improved the examination of intra group transactions especially in a cross border capacity.

	Turkey: With a change in the "Regulation on Financial Structures of the Insurance and Reinsurance and Retirement Companies" a weakening in the financial structure of the major equity owner to a degree that current and/or future commitments arising from contracts could not be met is also counted as one of the occasions of weakening in the financial structure of the company. Via this change a precaution against financial crisis was tried to be taken which may affect the insurance companies through their major equity owners whose financial structures were affected by the crisis. **USA**: Consideration is being given as to areas where insurance solvency regulation can be strengthened in response to "lessons learned from this crisis", but such decisions are being considered in the normal course of action. While some disclosure requirements for securities lending have been added, the more significant efforts (*e.g.*, group impacts, corporate governance) are being addressed through the Solvency Modernization Initiative. It should be noted that a new NAIC Working Group (Group Solvency Issues Working Group) that will consider possible changes to the NAIC Model Insurance Holding Company System Regulatory Act.
17b	**Ireland**: The Irish Financial Regulator is not the lead regulator of any insurance group. As part of the CEIOPS Coordination Committee meetings the Irish regulator shares information with other European regulators and responds to their initiatives and requests. **Italy**: The regulatory or supervisory measures in respect of groups have not been initiated specifically in the light of the crisis but of course are particularly relevant in crisis situations. In effect so far the Italian regulation on the supervision of groups has been effective and no major problems have occurred to the Italian groups. It is worth mentioning, inter alia, that the Italian Regulation gives to ISVAP the power to impose general and specific provisions at the top of the group (also when it is an insurance holding) concerning risk management, internal control mechanisms for the purposes of a stable and efficient management of the group. Moreover all the Italian groups are registered in the ISVAP's register of groups (available on ISVAP's website: www.isvap.it). **Switzerland**: In addition to the recent improvements as regards the relationship with other international supervisors we have also improved and intensified domestically our capture of data, frequency of this capture as well as more intensive analysis of the potential impacts and risks arising from this additional financial and operational information. In order to promote greater cooperation amongst our international colleagues regular 'reporting packs' with specific information to keep them informed especially in regards to the solvency, liquidity, risk and capital management practices of the entity at the group level were introduced. These have been found to assist greatly in frequent ad hoc teleconferences as well as setting a good foundation for more robust discussion at the annual supervisory college or coordination committee meetings. **Turkey**: Besides considering the weakening of the financial structure of major equity owners as a trigger to take a precaution, insurance supervisors from Insurance Supervision Board are entrusted in the companies whose major equity owners having financial trouble in abroad. In addition to closer scrutiny of activities, additional capital injections are demanded in light of the financial crisis. Meetings have been arranged with the companies which are deemed to be under risk due to the troubles their group companies abroad have been experiencing, and their current financial positions and concerns about future are discussed in detail. **USA**: Consideration is being given as to areas where insurance solvency regulation can be strengthened in response to "lessons learned from this crisis", but such decisions are being considered in the normal course of action. While some disclosure requirements for securities lending have been added, the more significant efforts (*e.g.*, group impacts, corporate governance) are being addressed through the Solvency Modernization Initiative. Its anticipated that all of the above will be considered, but the NAIC and state

| | insurance regulatory system is based primarily on a legal entity approach to regulation that walls off (protects) the consumer from other non insurance groups within the holding company structure. |

Table A.5. **Policy holder protection schemes, and restructuring and insolvency regime (if any)**

	20.a1 Policy holder protection scheme: life	20.a2 Policy holder protection scheme: non-life	20.b Measures have been taken to establish such schemes	20.c Measures to increase coverage amount	21. Granting of special government guarantees to policy holder funds/contracts	22. Financial education initiatives launched to address impacts of crisis on policy holders	26.a Special restructuring regime for insurers	26.b1 Is consideration is being given to having a special restructuring regime for insurers?	26.b2 Similar regime already in place for banks?	27. Restructurings, failures or insolvency linked to the crisis
Australia		●					●			
Austria	●					●	●			
Belgium		●			●			×	×	●
Canada	●	●			●					
Czech Rep.								×	×	
Finland		●						×	●	
Germany	●							×	●	
Greece		●								
Hungary			●					×	●	
Iceland							●			●
Ireland		●						×	●	
Italy						●		×	×	
Japan	●	●						×	●	●
Luxembourg								×	□	●
Mexico								×	×	
Netherlands	●							×	×	
Portugal		●				●	●			
Slovak Rep.								×	×	
Spain	●	●			●					
Sweden								×	●	
Switzerland							●			
Turkey	●	●					●		●	
USA	●	●		●		●	●		●	●
Russia		●				●			●	●

	Notes
20a	Policy holder protection compensation scheme for life companies recognizing the long term nature of their business and the difficulty in valuing embedded options. For general insurance the arrangements are new.

Belgium: Very limited.

Finland: For motor third party liability and workers compensation ("yhteistakuuerä" insurance company act (VYL) 9:5).

Germany: For life and health insurers.

Greece: Only for TPL motor insurance.

Netherlands: There is also protection in case of health insurance.

Spain: For the case of winding up of insurance undertakings.

Switzerland: According to the Swiss Insurance Supervision Law (ISL, Art 16.1) the insurance company shall establish adequate reserves to cover its entire commercial activities and shall guarantee claims arising from its insurance contracts by means of tied assets (Art 17.1). The amount of tied assets shall be equal to the technical reserves specified in Art. 16 plus a reasonable additional amount. The supervisory authority shall determine this additional amount. Tied assets are available primarily to satisfy claims of insured persons and must be covered at all times.

Turkey: In respect of the compulsory liability insurances imposed by the Insurance Law No:5684, Road Traffic Law No: 2918, Road Transportation Law No:4925 and compulsory insurances imposed by the Insurance Supervision Law No: 7397 which has been abolished by the Insurance Law No:5684 a Guarantee Account shall be established under the auspices of the Association of the Insurance and Reinsurance Companies of Turkey in order to cover the losses that arise as a result of the occurrence of the following conditions up to the related coverage amounts. a) personal injuries to a person where the insured cannot be identified, b) personal injuries caused by parties which do not have the required insurance coverage at the date the risk has occurred, c) personal injuries and damages to property for which the insurer is obliged to pay in the case of the withdrawal of his licenses in all branches permanently or his bankruptcy due to weakness in his financial situation, d) personal injuries for which the operator shall not be held responsible in accordance with the Road Traffic Law No: 2918 in an accident where the vehicle involved is stolen or seized by violence, e) the payments which shall be made by the Turkish Motor Insurance Bureau which deals with Green Card Insurance applications. Other than the Guarantee Account, guarantees that both the companies operating in life insurance branches and those operating in non life branches obliged to set aside in proportion with their commitments arising from the insurance policies can be considered as a policy holder protection compensation scheme. These guarantees are in fact a provision for the receivables of the policy holders and used in the case that the licenses of the insurance company in all branches it had been operating are cancelled due to a financial weakness, bankruptcy or liquidation.

USA: All 50 states and the District of Columbia have adopted laws that provide for a regulatory framework such as that contained in the NAIC's model act on the subject, to ensure the payment of policy holders' obligations subject to appropriate restrictions and limitations when a company is deemed insolvent. |
| 20a | **Australia**: There are specific legislative provisions which have the same effect. |

20b	**Netherlands**: Not in the Netherlands; however in Europe new discussions are starting up. **Portugal**: Work is being done at the EU level on insurance guarantee schemes. **Slovak Republic**: A consumer protection act in Slovak Republic is being prepared. There are some considerations during preparation of this act.
20c	**USA**: During December 2008, the NAIC adopted some coverage limits changes included within the Life & Health Insurance Guaranty Association Model Act and Property & Casualty Insurance Guaranty Association Model Act.
21	**Canada**: The crisis prompted the prudential regulator, Office of the Superintendent of Financial Institutions (OSFI) to review its capital requirements to assess if any changes where necessary to its rules. OSFI did not review the rules with a specific goal in mind in term of a quantitative impact (*e.g.*, making the capital test more or less conservative) but to make it more risk sensitive and to ensure that it is not pro-cyclical. OSFI has also made changes to ensure insurers hold increased levels of capital as the dates for specific insurance obligation payments become more proximate.
22	**Hungary**: The Hungarian Financial Supervisory Authority is continuously publishing information on the web site (www.pszaf.hu) in connection with the financial education of clients. **Netherlands**: There are general initiatives that also address further education of current and future policy holders. **Portugal**: The ISP has reinforced the explanations provided to policy holders that requested information about the nature and characteristics of insurance products, namely in the life insurance area, in order for them to take informed decisions on their investments. **Slovak Republic**: There are some considerations during preparation of the new consumer protection act. **Spain**: We have launched a new web site addressed to policy holders expressed in a easy language to understand, to inform them about their rights and obligations. **Turkey**: Instead of education initiatives, a number of conferences and seminars were organized and are being organized with the aim of informing and creating awareness in the sector about the crisis. They are generally launched to address and discuss the causes, results and potential impacts of the crisis on the insurance market as a whole. **USA**: NAIC and State Insurance Commissioners have issued many press releases and provided information on websites to educate the public on market conditions and consumer/policy holder considerations.
26a	**Australia**: Due to the nature of life insurance business the arrangements for this are somewhat different. For general business these arrangements are also new and were part of the legislative package introducing policy holder protection arrangements. **Austria**: § 104 VAG. **Germany**: Law is applicable for all financial institutions. **Mexico**: According to the General Law on Insurance Institutions and Mutual Societies (Ley General de Instituciones y Sociedades Mutualistas de Seguros, LGISMS), the government can intervene only in the liquidation proceedings of an insurance company.

	Portugal: The restructuring regime is not specific for insurance. **Switzerland**: The Swiss ISL contains a section on safeguards. Art. 51.2 points out that the supervisory authority shall take action as seems appropriate in order to protect the interests of the insured. In particular, it may: a. block an insurance company's free access to its own assets; b. order the deposit of assets or block them; c. assign powers entrusted to an executive body of an insurance company to a third party in full or in part; d. transfer the insurance portfolio and the associated tied assets to another insurance company subject to the latter's agreement; e. order the realisation of tied assets; f. demand the dismissal of persons entrusted with direction, supervision, control or management or that of the person(s) with general power of attorney or the accountable actuary and ban them from exercising further insurance activities for a maximum of five years; g. remove an insurance intermediary from the Register specified in Article 42. **USA**: All 50 states and the District of Columbia have adopted state laws that set forth a receivership scheme for the administration, by the insurance commissioner, of insurance companies found to be insolvent as set forth in the NAIC's Insurers Rehabilitation and Liquidation Model Act.
26b2.	**Australia**: The banking regime was introduced at the same time as the general insurance regime. **Canada**: Although no specific programmes have been established to support the capital position of financial institutions, governing financial institution statutes were amended to grant the government the authority to inject capital into federally regulated financial institutions. **Hungary**: Act CIV of 2008 on the strengthening of the stability of the financial system. **Ireland**: The Irish Government has nationalised one bank and injected redeemable preference share capital into two others. **USA**: Yes, U.S. Federal Bankruptcy Law.
27	**Belgium**: Ethias, Life insurer: problems of liquidity and compliance with solvency requirement. Solved with increase of capital by the government. **Iceland**: Two insurers do not meet the capital requirements. In one case, it can be attributed to the crisis. It is a non-life insurer. The former owners are bankrupt and it is now owned by the estate of Glitnir bank. The company will be sold and Glitnir bank will provide new assets to save the company. **Japan**: Small size life insurance company has failed due to their unique and aggressive investment strategies. **Luxembourg**: Insurance subsidiaries of banking groups in financial difficulties. **USA**: One receivership can be directly related to the financial crisis, which involved a small life insurer that went into rehabilitation. Additionally, there were seven restructurings prompted by insurers that did not involve regulatory actions, including four financial guaranty insurers, two mortgage guaranty insurers and one mid-sized life insurer.

Table A.6. Regulatory regime and process

	23. General gaps in the regulatory framework identified?	24. General improvements to the existing regulatory framework identified?	25. Have any waivers from regulatory requirements been granted that can be linked directly to the crisis?
Australia			
Austria			
Belgium			
Canada		●	
Czech Republic			
Finland			
Germany		●	
Greece			
Hungary	●		
Iceland			
Ireland		●	
Italy		●	
Japan			
Luxembourg	●		
Mexico			
Netherlands			
Portugal			
Slovak Republic			
Spain			
Sweden		●	
Switzerland			
Turkey			
USA			●
Russia		●	

	Notes
23	**Hungary**: There is a legal gap between the regulation of the investment funds and asset funds (*e.g.* unit-linked insurance investments). There is no compensation scheme in order to protect insurance policy holders in contrast with the other parts of the financial sector (e. g. banks, capital markets). **Ireland**: While no specific gaps in the regulatory framework for insurance have been identified, the Irish prime minister has announced that a new central banking commission will be established. It is expected that this will mean the reintegration of the prudential supervision functions from the Irish Financial Regulator into the Central Bank but no details are yet available. **Luxembourg**: Cash deposits with failing credit institutions.

	Netherlands: In the Netherlands supervision on insurance companies was already improved in the Dutch Financial supervisory Act, that came into force in 2007. This legislation will be evaluated in 2010. **Slovak Republic**: We have identified some regulatory gaps, but they does not relate to the crisis. **USA**: As noted previously, consideration is being given as to areas where insurance solvency regulation can be strengthened in response to "lessons learned from this crisis", but such decisions are being considered in the normal course of action, and none have been determined at this point in time.
24	**Canada**: Budget 2009 broadened the authority for the Minister of Finance to promote financial stability and provided a standby authority for the Government to inject capital into federally regulated financial institutions to support financial stability. **Ireland**: The Irish Financial Regulator has increased its monitoring of regulated firms. This has been done in several ways, inter alia, by survey, by additional information requests for variable annuity product writers, by closer scrutiny of insurers that are part of banking groups to assess contagion risk and insurers writing property linked business and/or variable annuities. The Irish Financial Regulator instigated a survey to encompass all regulated life and non-life insurance companies at 30 September 2008. Detailed information was requested on non-linked assets held by category, size and location, with details to be provided on templates supplied of fixed and variable interest securities, non EU government securities, deposits with credit institutions, guarantees given, bank exposures, structured credit products, AIG and Lehman exposures, technical provisions and solvency margins. The Financial Regulator also asked for a qualitative statement outlining what stress testing each company has carried out in relation to its exposures and how it proposes to deal with any challenges it faces. The Financial Regulator had already requested all companies to begin electronic quarterly reporting commencing with data for 31 December 2008. This online reporting will enhance and expedite the analysis and intensive monitoring of data. **Italy**: A draft regulatory on index linked products is under consultation. It lays down new rules on "permitted linked". The new rules will go together with the provisions already stated in 2003 (ISVAP Circular n. 507), which clearly established the prohibition for "index-linked" products to use credit derivatives or asset-backed securities as reference parameters in these kind of contracts. **Netherlands**: The Solvency II QIS exercises are also used in the supervision. It gives further information for the supervisor and it gives insurance companies an incentive to prepare for Solvency II. **USA**: As noted previously, consideration is being given as to areas where insurance solvency regulation can be strengthened in response to "lessons learned from this crisis", but such decisions are being considered in the normal course of action, and none have been determined at this point in time.
25	**Finland**: Yes, for 1st pillar statutory pension schemes. **Italy**: Except for what already specified on ISVAP regulation 28. **USA**: Permitted practices have been extended by certain state insurance regulators under specific circumstances. These accounting deviations differ from insurer to insurer, but ultimately impact capital. The impacts on capital and surplus and net income are disclosed in the Notes to Financial Statements of the relevant insurers' public statutory filings.

| 28 | Additional comments

Russia: Among planned measures in Russia:

- the obligation of insurers to provide the support of solvency margin on permanent basis not only during the reporting period

- the inclusion of subordinate loan to the actual solvency margin account if the period of subordinate loan is not less than 5 years and subordinate loan contract has the provision of early termination inability

- the growth of the basic solvency margin indicator for definite insurers

- the margin reduction not more than 25 % for the insurers who have S&P, Moody's Investors Service, Fitch Rating not lower then BBB, Baa2, BBB and whose actual margin indicator override the basic more than 35% for the last 10 years

- new requirement for contract commitments which could be not exceed 10% of the insurer' own funds |
|---|---|

Table A.7. Intervention in credit insurance markets

(Protection for Domestic and/or Export Receivables)

DOM = Domestic
EXP = Export
SFI = State financial institution
SEA = State export agency

	DOM				Comment (Reference to "indirect" means that provision is through private-sector)	EXP				Comment (Reference to "indirect" means that provision is through private-sector)
		Top-up	Generalised	Other			Top-up	Generalised	Other	
		New coverage					New Coverage			
Australia										
Austria						●	●	●		Direct by SEA and indirect through reinsurance by SEA
Belgium	●	●			Indirect using SFI	●	●			Indirect using SFI; for EEA only
Canada	●	●			Indirect using SEA; direct SEA provision to automotive sector					
Czech R.						●			●	Increased state risk retention (to 99%)
Denmark						●	●	●		Indirect: reinsu-rance via SEA
Finland						●	●			Direct by SEA
France	●	●	●		Indirect using SFI (CCR)	●	●	●		Indirect
Germany	●	●			Indirect	●	●			Indirect via industry consortium
Greece										
Hungary										
Ireland										
Italy										
Japan						●	●			
Korea										
Luxem-bourg						●	●			Indirect via SEA
Mexico										
Nether-lands						●	●			Indirect via reinsurance
New Zealand						●	●	●		Direct and indirect via reinsurance through SEA.

Country									
Norway					Short-term credit insurance already provided by SEA				Short-term credit insurance already provided by SEA for all countries
Poland									
Portugal						●	●		Indirect
Slovak R.									
Spain	●	●			Indirectly through SFI (CCS)	●		●	Indirectly through pools
Switzerland									
Sweden									
Turkey									
U.K.	●	●			Indirect				
U.S.						●		●	Reduced premium rates and increased coverage for SMEs

	Notes
Country	**Actions to Support Credit Insurance Markets – OECD Country Initiatives**
Australia	No known changes or initiatives.
Austria	Austria has temporarily extended its export credit insurance cover to marketable risks. Under this scheme, the Austrian Federal Ministry of Finance provides, through its agent Oesterreichische Kontrollbank, short term export credit insurance cover to exporters and reinsurance facilities to private insurance companies that are temporarily confronted with unavailability of cover in the private market for financially sound transactions as a result of the financial crisis.. The scheme involves: (a) the direct provision of short-term export-credit insurance to exporters (there is no limitation regarding the groups of products or sectors that can be covered, but there is a requirement that the exporter must face a withdrawal of private cover first before applying for state credit insurance); and (b) the provision of reinsurance to credit insurers, permitting the topping up of insurance in cases where existing credit limits of policy holders have been reduced by credit insurers or where new credit limits have been imposed. For direct cover, state coverage is primarily 80% of the total transaction value, but depending on the quality of the risk the coverage could range up to 90%; for reinsurance, the maximum cover by the state is either 70% or 80%. The scheme is scheduled to expire at the end of 2010. See: http://ec.europa.eu/community_law/state_aids/comp-2009/n434-09.pdf
Belgium	In July 2009, the federal government decided to establish a system of complementary credit insurance called Belgacap ("Complément d'Assurance-Credit Public", or public credit insurance supplement), distributed by private-sector credit insurers and guaranteed by the Belgian state under specific conditions. Belgacap provides complementary coverage to Belgian firms that were covered by credit insurance as of 1 January 2009 but that have seen a reduction in coverage, and to those firms whose application for credit insurance had only been partially accepted as of that same date (and, specifically for the latter, only for coverage of invoices not issued as of the date of the request for coverage). Belgium's Participation Fund, a federal financial institution, administers Belgacap.

	Belgacap covers only receivables debts owed by counterparties established within the European Economic Area (EEA), and cannot be used in conjunction with any other similar system of complementary coverage. Belgacap comes into effect once a credit insurer accepts an application for coverage. There are limitations on the complementary coverage provided under Belgacap: - It is, combined with the coverage provided by the credit insurer, no greater than the coverage initially requested by the firm - No greater than the coverage provided by the credit insurer if no request for extra coverage was made; - No greater than EUR1.5 million for small to medium-sized enterprises (SMEs) - No greater than EUR3 million for firms other than SMEs - The applicable premium rate must be greater than the premium rate set for the coverage by the credit insurer (commission deducted) As suggested above, no Belgacap coverage is possible in the event of the termination and/or refusal of coverage by the private-sector credit insurer. The premium to be paid by the firm is 0.50% of the value of the complementary coverage provided by the credit insurer, paid quarterly (coverage provided is for a period of 3 months, and is renewable). The guarantee provided by the state is capped at EUR300 million worth of receivables insured under Belgacap. The guarantee can only be accessed once the primary coverage proves itself to be insufficient to meet the claim. Belgacap was expected to terminate on 8 January 2010 (six-month duration), but has been extended until 31 December 2010.
Canada	The federal government established a **Business Credit Availability Program** (involving of at least CDN$5 billion in additional loans and other forms of credit support) to provide *financing*, *credit insurance*, and *contract insurance and bonding* to viable, creditworthy companies facing problems with access to credit. Two state-owned corporations, the Business Development Bank of Canada (BDC) and Export Development Corporation (EDC) are administering this program. The EDC, which normally provides financing and export credit insurance, received a temporary two-year broadening of its legal mandate to undertake domestic financing and insurance. The BCAP has three components: *1. Financing*: EDC expanded its *Export Guarantee Program* to the domestic market in order to make loans directly to eligible businesses or provide guarantees to support bank loans to these businesses. EDC's support will focus on trade-oriented businesses that might not normally meet its traditional "exporter" criteria" but where the organisation can leverage its expertise. Some sectors are not eligible for assistance: retail, wholesale, tourism, entertainment, and real estate. Businesses with less $50 million in revenues that are not already EDC customers are referred to the BDC for this type of support. *2. Credit insurance*: EDC will provide reinsurance to private credit insurers to enable incremental domestic credit insurance coverage. This domestic-oriented initiative will complement EDC's traditional role as provider of export trade credit insurance. EDC received

	CDN$1 billion to match additional private sector coverage (*i.e.*, 50/50 risk-sharing), therefore potentially enabling up to $2 billion in new direct credit insurance capacity. Reinsurance will provided only for credit insurance coverage of businesses that already have such coverage and are seeking additional capacity but cannot obtain it under current market conditions. The government opted to use reinsurance as its method of intervention based on the view that it could leverage existing market expertise and provider relationships with existing customers. There are no restrictions on sectors for this coverage. EDC is also providing direct credit insurance coverage to the automotive sector. EDC already provides short-term export credit insurance. 3. ***Contract insurance and bonding***: EDC is also providing reinsurance coverage to domestic surety companies (50/50 risk sharing) as well as guarantees to banks to support incremental domestic bonding. EDC's efforts are focussed on new bonding requirements that exceed existing guarantees or surety bonds, not existing guarantees or surety bonds; moreover, businesses covered must already be an existing client of the surety company or bank. There are no sectoral restrictions on eligibility; however, EDC's focus will be on guarantees related to EDC's experience, namely contract performance.
Czech Republic	The Export Guarantee and Insurance Corporation (EGAP) has, in light of the crisis: - Seen its authorised insurance capacity raised from CZK120 billion to CZK150 billion; - Temporarily increased export credit insurance cover of the risk of non-payment of all types of export credits from 95 per cent to 99 per cent; and, - Reduced substantially the price of insurance for "manufacturing risk", where an exporter is insured against the risk of losses resulting from cancellation or interruption of a contract on the part of the foreign importer. EGAP has developed a product that is expected to insure short-term transactions that were previously insured by commercial credit insurers. The launch of this product is dependent on approval by the European Commission. (See www.egap.cz; TAD/PG(2009)17/FINAL)
Denmark	In March 2009, the Danish government set up a reinsurance framework agreement with private-sector export credit insurers to address the withdrawal of the private sector from export credit insurance, particularly in respect of short-term export risk (less than 2 years). The programme is targeted to Danish companies and is intended to cover risks on transactions for which private insurers have withdrawn their cover or for which coverage has expired. The reinsurance agreements with the private sector are valid for one year and cannot exceed DKK10 billion per annum; there is a possibility of their extension until the end of 2010. The reinsurance programme is administered by Eksport Kredit Fonden (EKF), the Danish public export agency. To be eligible under the reinsurance programme, exporters must hold a credit insurance policy on standard terms with a private credit insurer. Therefore, new exporters must apply for a private credit insurance policy before benefitting from the programme. In addition, reinsurance is provided only for export transactions with credit terms of up to 180 days. Furthermore, export transactions must take place with a buyer who: (a) has had no registered payment default within the preceding six months; (b) has not triggered any claim payment by an insurance company; and (c) does not have a very high probability of default. This reinsurance is offered under two different schemes, both involving cooperation with private-sector credit insurance companies: - ***Top-up coverage***: Under this scheme, EKF offers top-up coverage, *i.e.*, EKF offers Danish exporters extra coverage on selected foreign buyers where private credit insurers

	cannot offer full coverage. The risk retained by the insured in the contracts corresponds to that of the standard policy of the credit insurer. The premium rate for top-up guarantees is 0.5% of revenue (same for all export markets); the minimum premium rate is that of the standard policy. • **Quota share coverage**: EKF offers quota share coverage, *i.e.* EKF can offer Danish companies coverage on selected buyers with sound risks but for which the private sector is not able to cover. The risk retained by the insured in the contracts is 15%. The premium rate for quota share coverage is determined by country category: 0.9% of revenue for the best countries, 1.2% for the intermediate category, and 1.4% for countries in category III. | Price for quota share	Country category I	Country category II	Country category IIII
---	---	---	---
Risk retained by insured (percent)	15	15	15
Premium (percent of contract value)	0.9	1.2	1.4	 The private trade credit insurers are responsible for managing claims. Losses are distributed between the relevant credit insurance company and EKF according to a special distribution arrangement agreed between the parties (though EKF takes the largest share of the loss). (See http://www.ekf.dk/Reinsurance)
Finland	Finnvera (state export guarantee agency) has temporarily extended its export credit insurance cover to marketable risks. This extension will take the form of a Credit Risk Guarantee (*i.e.,,* insurance of risks of receivables; in simplified form for SMEs it is called the Export Receivables Guarantee) and a Buyer Credit Guarantee (where a lender partially provides credit to an importer instead of by the exporter), both of which cover exclusively the risks emanating from the possibility that the importer does not pay for the received export goods and/or services. Maximum coverage for Finnvera is 90%, with the remaining 10% retained by the exporter/lender. Finnvera will provide cover only for those exporters that have been refused cover with a private insurer or whose credit limit with a private insurer has been significantly reduced (at least a 25% reduction). Finnvera will charge the same premium rates as those applied to short-term export credit insurance in the non-marketable countries. The premium is charged up front as a flat percentage of the export declared, which varies according to the length of the risk period. This special export credit insurance will be in force until 31 December 2010. As of October 2009, the total value of the guarantees granted was EUR 32 million. In addition, the overall maximum exposure limit for export credit guarantees was increased in June 2009 to EUR 12.5 billion. (See www.finnvera.fi; *Letter from European Commission on State Aid N 258/09 – Finland: Short-term export-credit insurance* http://ec.europa.eu/community_law/state_aids/comp-2009/n258-09.pdf)
France	Three temporary programmes have been established by the French government to support **private credit insurance markets**, both for domestic business as well as for export-oriented business. All three programmes involve some sort of state reinsurance or guarantee mechanism: • The *Complément d'Assurance-crédit Public* (CAP) is intended to ensure the continued

availability of credit insurance for suppliers dealing with small to medium-sized purchasers (less than EUR1.5 billion in revenues). Businesses that find their credit insurance coverage cut by private-sector credit insurers due to their exposures to these types of purchasers can obtain a CAP guarantee that provides coverage up to 50% of the original coverage amount (as of 1 October 2008). This program allows businesses to retain 100% of their original coverage so long as private insurers do not cut their coverage below 50% of the original amount; any coverage reduction greater than 50% means a reduction in CAP coverage to ensure 50/50 risk-sharing with the private sector. CAP amounts insured by credit insurers are reinsured directly with the Caisse Centrale des Reassurances (CCR), France's state-owned natural catastrophe reinsurer. CAP is offered on a 3-month renewable basis, with higher-than-average-market premiums charged (1.5% of receivables versus an average market rate of 1%; 0.3% is given to the credit insurer for commercialisation and brokerage of the CAP, 1.2% to the CRR) to reflect the risk undertaken by the CCR. The CAP became operational in December 2008. The state's guarantee to the CCR for the CAP is capped at EUR10 billion and is expected to expire on 31 December 2009.

With the establishment of the CAP programme, the private-sector credit insurers agreed to the following commitments as a means to promote confidence between credit insurers and their clients, and improve transparency in the market, namely:

− Systematically propose the CAP to firms;

− Not reduce, globally, the percentage of receivables of French firms that they insure over the next six months;

− Provide to the government, every month, statistics on the level of insured receivables, with specification of the extent to which the receivables of small and medium-sized businesses are insured;

− Re-examine, within 5 days, any file transmitted to the French national credit mediator regarding a firm experiencing a cut-back in coverage;

− Not proceed with cutting back coverage on a sectoral basis with taking into account the individual circumstances of each firm;

− Systematically provide a rationale for any decision to modify coverage for any given risk

− Provide necessary explanations to those businesses seeking information on how the credit insurer's evaluation of the individual business is evolving.

• The *CAP+*, established in May 2009, responded to concerns about: (i) cancelled credit insurance coverage – thus disabling a previously insured business' access to CAP; and (ii) the inability of non-insured businesses to access any credit insurance to protect themselves against new-found risks posed by the financial crisis. Coverage under CAP+ is provided to businesses transacting with small or medium-sized businesses (same revenue threshold as CAP) that have seen their coverage fully withdrawn or that are seeking to secure coverage, and whose default rate over a 1 year period is expected to lie between 2 to 6% (deemed to be a low enough default rate to avoid undue exposure by the state to firm insolvency risk, but a high enough rate to prevent CAP+ from insuring risks that can be covered by industry).

The CAP+ is organised differently from the CAP. It is set up as a credit insurance guarantee fund capable of covering EUR5 billion worth of receivables on an annualised basis, and is administered by the CCR. Insured parties retain 20% of losses, with the remaining losses retained by the state, through the CCR, up to a EUR600 million threshold on the CCR's share of losses; in excess of this threshold, credit insurers then absorb 10% of losses. The private-sector credit insurers are responsible for the commercialisation of CPA+ but do not

	retain any risk (subject to the threshold mentioned above); instead, all amounts insured under CAP+ are transferred directly to the account of the guarantee fund. The French government has to date committed to injecting EUR200 million into the CAP+ guarantee fund. The level of coverage that can be obtained is determined by the applicant, but a ceiling is placed on the amount of credit insurance per counterparty (EUR200,000 for less risky counterparties, EUR100,000 for riskier counterparties), with the maximum indemnity per insured business being EUR3 million. Credit insurance is provided only on 3-month renewable basis and costs an annual 2.4% of receivables (0.6% is given to credit insurers for commercialisation and management of the guarantee, and 1.8% to the CCR). At least 20% of the risk must be retained by insured business as a means to align incentives. The CAP+ was seen as a temporary measure and is due to expire on 31 December 2009. • *CAP Export* was established in October 2009 to support small and medium-sized enterprises (similar threshold as in CAP/CAP+) based in France and exporting abroad. CAP Export effectively provides two types of guarantees on a 3-month renewable basis, similar to CAP and CAP+: as with CAP, it can provide coverage to exporters that have seen a reduction in their export credit insurance coverage, up to 50% of their original coverage; in addition, CAP+ provides coverage for exporters that have lost their coverage entirely or for exporters seeking coverage but unable to obtain it, and where the probability of default of the counterparty over the next year lies between 2 and 6%. CAP Export is administered by the private-sector credit insurers and is supported by a state guarantee; Coface, a private-sector credit insurer, manages the risk for the state guarantor, that is, the French Treasury. *Additional notes*: – Credit insurance covers roughly one quarter of receivables in France, or approximately EUR320 billion. A majority of risks covered by credit insurance are linked to small and medium-sized companies. – A private-sector credit insurer, Coface, has noted that for every 5 euros of short-term credit given to firms, 1 euro comes from banks while 4 euros come from suppliers (*RiskAssur – hebdo*, 30 March 2009) – Building and public works sector is seen as particularly hard hit by non-payment for goods and services rendered in the crisis. – Take-up of CAP and CAP+ as of 9 October 2009: EUR448 million guaranteed receivables under CAP and 14,986 activated files; EUR491 million guaranteed receivables under CAP+ and 23,620 activated files. Amounts insured on average are relatively modest: EUR30,000 for CAP and EUR20,000 for CAP+. Roughly 38,000 commercial relationships have reportedly been protected by CAP and CAP+ (see www.minefe.gouv.fr).
Germany	The federal government has established a temporary export credit insurance scheme that offers state short-term export credit insurance to German exporters that are confronted, due to the crisis, with unavailability of trade credit insurance cover in the private market for financially sound transactions. This scheme involves the extension of the already existing state export credit guarantee scheme. The existing public scheme offers state insurance for short-, medium- and long-term export transactions. However, in case of the short-term transactions, public cover was offered only for exports to countries defined as non-marketable. The state-sponsored insurance will be offered by Euler Hermes Bund to companies established in Germany, with no limitations regarding to the groups of products or sectors covered. That said, coverage will be offered for four main types of products: Whole Turnover Policy (APG) (or in simplified form for SMEs as Export Whole Turnover Policy light), Supplier Credit Cover (single or revolving) and Manufacturing Risk Cover. The standard policy offered by the private

	credit insurers in Germany is the whole-turnover policy, where all exports by the company are covered up to an agreed turnover limit.

Exporters will, in principle be required to retain 10% of the risk, but they may apply for a reduction to 5% (this reduction of risk retention by the exporter is available only until 31 December 2010, though the government reserves the right to increase the exporter's retention to a maximum of 35% should the risk assessment of the buyer identify a heightened risk). The remaining risks will be covered by the government. Euler Hermes does not retain any risk related to the coverage provided under the scheme.

Export transactions that are insured must be justifiable in terms of the commercial and political risk involved. These include the financial strength and economic policies of the country concerned, as well as macro-economic and political factors, as well as the foreign buyer's creditworthiness and payment record. The scheme will not be applied to buyers in economic difficulties or to buyers with a weak or insufficient solvency.

The scheme will be administrated on behalf of the federal government by a private-sector consortium consisting of Euler Hermes Kreditversicherungs-AG (Euler Hermes Bund) and PricewaterhouseCoopers AG WPG – the same consortium that manages the public German export credit insurance system. The Consortium will receive the applications for cover, conduct risk assessment, take the decisions to provide coverage on behalf of the state for export contracts up to EUR 5 million (or prepare decisions on applications for consideration at the meetings of the Interministerial Committee (IMC) for contracts exceeding this threshold), and handle claims. The Consortium will receive around EUR 55 – 68 million for administration, depending, inter alia, on the volume covered transactions.

A strict "Chinese wall" will exist between the activities of Euler Hermes as a private credit insurer (Euler Hermes Privat) and the Consortium (in particular Euler Hermes Bund). This translates to separation of accounts and administration between those parties. Moreover, no exchange of credit information on individual foreign buyers takes place. In addition, Euler Hermes Privat is not in a position to shift risks which are difficult to accept on own account to the Consortium.

The same system of premium rates will be applied as the one, which defines the level of premium for the State insurance cover for the non-marketable countries in the normal market conditions. The premium to be paid by the exporter for the insurance cover within the notified measure varies according to the category of the country, in which the buyer is based, his creditworthiness, nature of risk covered and the type of the policy.

The annual remuneration due to the Consortium for the administration of the public scheme with the total budget of up to EUR 117 billion is estimated at around EUR 55 – 68 million and depends, inter alia, on the volume covered transactions. This corresponds to all administrative costs and a management fee for the Consortium related to the administration of the whole State export credit guarantee scheme covering both non-marketable and temporarily non-marketable risks.

The public short-term export credit insurance cover is available to all exporters established in Germany until 31 December 2010.

In December 2009, the federal government set up a guarantee scheme that offers top-up cover in the trade credit insurance. The guarantee scheme has a total volume of up to 7,5 billion EUR and will expire on 31 December 2010. |
| **Greece** | No known changes or initiatives. |

Hungary	No known changes or initiatives.
Ireland	After reviewing the benefits and costs of introducing a short-term state short-term export credit insurance scheme, a decision was recently made that such a scheme should not be adopted for cost and effectiveness reasons.
Italy	No known changes or initiatives.
Japan	In response to the financial crisis, the following measures have been introduced, amongst others (see http://www.nexi.go.jp/e/topics-s/ts_090113.html): ***1. Financial support for business by Japanese overseas subsidiaries***: The following support will be available through the end of March 2010 by the Nippon Export and Investment Insurance (NEXI) to meet the needs of Japanese overseas subsidiaries: • *Support for working capital*: Overseas Untied Loan Insurance (OULI) will be available to loan financing for Japanese overseas subsidiaries as their working capital with one-year term or longer (currently OULI is available to loan financing for investment capital only for a two-year term or longer). • *Increase of commercial risk cover*: The percentage of commercial risk cover of OULI to loan financing for Japanese overseas subsidiaries will be increased up to 90% from the current level of 50%. • *Cover with parent company guarantee*: OULI will be extended to loan financing to Japanese overseas subsidiaries based on the credit worthiness of their parent companies if guarantees are provided by the parent companies. ***2. Insurance cover for supplier's credit***: The Japan Bank for International Cooperation (JBIC) launched, as an exceptional temporary measure, a facility for export credit insurance, to be made available for exports to developing countries with deferred payment. Loans will also be made available for investment projects in developing countries through major Japanese companies (overseas investment loans). Separately, JBIC launched a financing facility that provides loans and guarantees to Japanese firms (including small and medium-sized enterprises) to finance their business operations in industrial countries - normally such facilities are provided only for firms operating in developing countries. Eligible businesses are defined as: "the business categories determined by the competent minister to belong to the industries that are experiencing significant difficulties in promoting the government policy of maintaining their international competitiveness due to the global financial turmoil". (See www.jbic.go.jp).
Korea	No known changes or initiatives. Increased support has been provided for export trade credit insurance, *e.g.*, increase of the annual export insurance limit for the Korean Export Insurance Corporation to $170bn for 2009 from $130bn for 2008. (http://www.berneunion.org.uk/pdf/PressRelease19November2008.pdf)
Luxembourg	Luxembourg has established a temporary "individual top-up" export credit insurance scheme. The coverage provided under this scheme complements basic export credit insurance taken out with private credit insurers. The government-backed export credit agency, Ducroire Luxembourg ("Ducroire"), will provide buyers with higher coverage limits than those offered by commercial credit insurers where there is evidence that credit insurers have reduced their limits (Ducroire normally provides medium and long-term credit insurance and short-term credit insurance for

non-marketable-risk countries with a state guarantee, and short-term export credit insurance without a state guarantee for marketable-risk countries). Ducroire has been authorised to cover, on behalf of the State, up to EUR 25 million of coverage. This scheme is due to expire on 31 December 2010.

The percentage of cover applying to the claims covered is laid down and applied by the basic credit insurance company when calculating its indemnity. The sum insured per debtor is the amount of the complementary coverage provided in addition to the coverage provided by the private credit insurer. The indemnity is calculated according to the rules applied by the basic credit insurance company.

Ducroire will be directly involved in decision-making on coverage. Acting on behalf of the Luxembourg authorities, Ducroire will, when assessing the risk of an operation, adopt a similar approach to that taken before the crisis by private insurance companies when deciding to grant cover. In this context, cover will not be provided for a firm that would not have been insured by a private company prior to the crisis.

The private credit insurer covers the initial losses up to the limit insured by it. The state will cover only the losses exceeding this limit, up to the limit insured in the top-up policy. In order to determine the applicable limits, the Luxembourg authorities defined a methodology based on the situation of policy holders:

- *Undertakings insured before 1 September 2008*: The credit limit exceeding the limit of the basic credit insurance is established on an individual basis; the ceiling is the limit which was granted before 1 September 2008 provided that the undertaking had an insurance policy before that date.

- *Undertakings insured after 1 September 2008*: The complementary cover can also apply to an undertaking not insured before 1 September 2008. If the coverage decision by the credit insurance company is not satisfactory for the firm, it can ask for top-up cover. Ducroire will then take an individual decision on the basis of a file containing a record of the firm's turnover with the buyer, the buyer's payment history, details relating to the private credit insurance company's decision and all other information which the firm considers important or which Ducroire deems necessary. The conditions governing cover will be identical to those in the basic credit insurance and the premium rates will be calculated in the same way as for firms insured before 1 September 2008.

- *Undertakings unable to obtain insurance*: In principle, the coverage to be granted is applicable only if the firm has a private credit insurance policy. If an undertaking that was not insured before 1 September 2008 is refused access to private credit insurance, Ducroire will examine the case individually and will ask the firm to provide evidence that it took the necessary steps to obtain cover from several credit insurance companies. If the firm can provide evidence that private credit insurance companies refused to offer insurance, then a special investigation is carried out to find out the reasons for their refusal and to take a decision on the case. Before taking a decision is made on granting cover, however, Ducroire must contact the private credit insurers to encourage them to provide an insurance policy.

The top-up premium costs three times the basic insurance premium for the amount covered if declared insolvency is covered, and at least 1.5% per year. If the policy holder wishes to cover alleged insolvency, the minimum premium rate rises to 4% per year. The premium is payable in advance. The cover last for 3 months and is renewable; however, a new application for the granting of credit must be made in order to renew the cover. If this accepted, a new quarterly premium is paid. |
| **Mexico** | No known changes or initiatives. |

Netherlands	The Dutch scheme provides short-term export-credit insurance coverage to Dutch exporters that are confronted with temporary unavailability of cover in the private market. The scheme reinsures the topping up of coverage limits by private-sector credit insurers. This topping up will be available for: • existing credit limits when they are reduced by credit insurers; or • new credit limits given by credit insurers, but which are lower than the requested amount by the insured company. The decision on the provision of top-up cover on an individual basis is left to the discretion of credit insurers. The maximum exposure of the State to the total risk of export transactions assumed under the scheme is EUR 1.5 billion at any point in time. Top-up coverage that expires can, however, be reused, which means that the total amount insured under the scheme could be higher than EUR 1.5 billion. Only specific export transactions are eligible under the scheme based on their risk category. This safeguard aims to prevent private credit insurers from transferring following two types of risks to the state: risks that can still be supported in the private market without state support; or bad risks relating to unsound transactions that would not find coverage in the private market in the normal market conditions. The short-term export credit insurance is provided by the government in the form of a reinsurance facility. There is a Framework Agreement between the government and all the participating credit insurers in which the principles of the short-term export credit insurance scheme are laid out. Each credit insurer has entered into a separate reinsurance agreement with the state in concordance with the Framework Agreement. With credit insurers executing the scheme for the state, their underwriting practices ultimately affects the risks reinsured by the state. The maximum possible top-up provided by the government is 100% of the cover offered by the credit insurer. The reinsurance facility will therefore never take on more than 50% of the total risk on any buyer (and possibly lower if customers do not ask for a full top-up). The total amount of reinsured cover provided to a policy holder shall at no point in time exceed the lower of: (i) EUR 1 million per policy holder or buyer; or (ii) 50% per credit limit provided to the relevant policy holder by the credit insurer, *i.e.* the sum of limits under primary and top-up policy. In addition to the limitations of individual transactions, there is an overall coverage limitation per buyer of EUR 2.5 million. The risk retention rate of the policy holder is the same as for the underlying private policy. Premiums for the top-up policy are paid every three months, and equals 1.5% of the limit provided during these three months. There is no differentiation in the level of premiums as far as period of coverage, country risk or buyer risk is concerned. Exporters must pay an administration and handling fees per top-up policy. The premium due by the credit insurers to the state in respect of reinsurance provided is equal to 1.5% minus a discount of 35% (= "management fee"). The initial mandate of the reinsurance scheme was until the end of 2009. The facility was extended until 31 December 2010. The facility will, in 2010, become less expensive as the premium rate will drop from 1.5% to 1.0% per quarter; furthermore, the terms and conditions will be changed in order to permit more firms to qualify for the scheme. It has been observed that, with respect to trade credit insurance, problems seem to arise for credit insurance on very large companies, where insurance companies may reach their limit in terms of the exposure they can assume for any one single entity.

	(From Letter from European Commission on State Aid N 409/2009 – The Netherlands: Short-term export-credit insurance http://ec.europa.eu/community_law/state_aids/comp-2009/n409-09.pdf)
New Zealand	There do not appear to be any specific initiatives on domestic credit insurance. Rather, the focus has been on export trade credit insurance. The New Zealand Export Credit Office's (NZECO) established, in February 2009, a NZ$50 million facility that provides a short-term trade credit guarantee for exporters or insurers against defaults on contracts with payment terms of less than 360 days. The facility is provided until June 2011. The creation of the facility was accompanied by a change in the legal mandate of the NZECO to support the private sector's provision of short-term trade credit assistance. To qualify, exporters and/or their banks must confirm that the private sector is unable to provide or continue to support the export transaction(s) on reasonable terms and conditions. The export transaction must also be commercially sound with a credit-worthy buyer or bank. The government extended this facility in June by NZ$100 million given strong demand. As a complementary arrangement to NZECO's short-term trade guarantee, NZECO and Euler Hermes Trade Credit agreed, in July 2009, on top-up cover arrangement to assist New Zealand exporters that were already customers of Euler Hermes. This arrangement enables an exporter to obtain an excess layer of trade credit insurance underwritten by NZECO; this top-up coverage may replace primary cover that Euler Hermes has partially withdrawn on an exporter's buyer, or provide a top-up layer of cover where Euler Hermes has only partially approved the buyer limit requested by the exporter. NZECO's top-up coverage must not exceed the level of the reduced or partially approved primary level of cover (*i.e.*, 50/50 cost-sharing). For example, if an exporter has primary cover on a foreign buyer reduced from NZ$800,000 to NZ$300,000, then the maximum top-up cover is NZ$300,000; or, if an exporter applies for a NZ$800,000 primary cover limit on a buyer but receives approval for only NZ$500,000, the maximum top-up cover is $500,000. An exporter seeking NZECO's top-up cover must apply through Euler Hermes, which has the responsibility of arranging and administering this top-up cover on NZECO's behalf. The NZECO is responsible for assessing applications, approvals, and calculating the premium for each application for top-up cover; an exporter will receive a formal quotation from NZECO. If the exporter accepts and pays the up-front premium to the NZECO, then the NZECO Top-up Policy as well as Top-up Permitted Limits in relation to each foreign buyer will be issued. Euler Hermes administers claims on NZECO's behalf ; however, the NZECO makes the final decision regarding acceptance of a claim in relation to top-up coverage. The government has also provided $200 million more in trade guarantees to extend three trade credit guarantee and bond products: extending the US surety bond product by NZ$70 million to NZ$170 million (companies selling products to US government bodies must provide such a bond) ; extending the export credit guarantee product by NZ$100 million to NZ$315 million, which enables exporters to offer overseas buyers repayment terms longer than 360 days and covers them in event of default ; and extending the general contracts bond product by NZ$30 million to NZ$75 million. This is a guarantee to an exporter's bank that enables the bank to issue a bond required as part of the exporter's contract in a situation where they lack collateral. (See www.nzeco.govt.nz).
Norway	The state-owned Norwegian Guarantee Institute for Export Credits (GIEK) covers Norwegian exporters' credit risks. GIEK's objective is to promote Norwegian exports by issuing credit guarantees on behalf of the Norwegian government. The GIEK "General Scheme" is the GIEK's main line of activity. These mainly involve guarantees issued to lenders; most of the larger

	guarantees cover long-term credits in which GIEK shares the risk with lenders or other banks. Given the financial crisis, the Norwegian government has increased GIEK's exposure limits from 60 to 80 billion kroner, with the option of further increasing its guarantee limit to 110 billion kroner.

GIEK's wholly owned subsidiary company, GIEK Kredittforsikring AS (GIEK Credit Insurance), provides credit insurance coverage in respect of both foreign and domestic buyers (up to 2 years). The standard credit insurance policy covers up to 90 per cent of losses due to buyers becoming insolvent, going bankrupt, or being unwilling to pay. GIEK Credit Insurance reinsures its political and commercial risks outside the OECD countries through a reinsurance agreement with the parent company, GIEK.

In fall 2008, an exceptionally high number of enquiries and applications for coverage were made to GIEK Credit Insurance, reflecting worsened availability of short-term credit. Applications were made by large, well-known companies and organisations that had largely been without insurance previously (*i.e.*, self-insured) or that had difficulties obtaining cover from private companies.

(See http://www.giek.no) |
Poland	No known changes or initiatives.
Portugal	A "top up cover" insurance protocol was approved to support export credit transactions for enterprises to be covered against an additional credit risk, with State guarantee extended through a Portuguese Mutual Guarantee Companies (in the Portuguese acronym SGM) available for risks located in Portugal or in other OECD countries, to compensate the decreased limits of credits attributed within the framework of a credit insurance policy. This facility is available to all export credit insurance companies operating in Portugal, under the same conditions. This facility will expire on 31 December 2010. (See TAD/PG(2009)17/FINAL and www.spgm.pt)
Slovak R.	No known changes or initiatives.
Spain	The Spanish government has undertaken two initiatives in relation to credit insurance, one oriented toward the domestic market, the other oriented to the export market:

- In March 2009, the Spanish government introduced a special measure to reinforce the capacity of the private credit insurance market in Spain. The government authorized the Consorcio de Compensación de Seguros (CCS), a state-owned reinsurer responsible for compensating insurers covering extraordinary risks, to reinsure credit and bond risks covered by domestic credit and bond insurers. The value of transactions supported by this initiative could reach EUR40 billion.

  The CCS and UNESPA (the Spanish insurance association, Associación Empresarial del Seguro) reached an agreement by which EUR20 billion worth of credit transactions could be supported in 2009. The CCS agreed to cover 85% of losses on credit insurance contracts insofar as the loss rate on these contracts lies between 85% and 130% of premiums paid. This could lead to a loss of up to EUR200 million, with the net loss being no more than EUR170 million for the CCS. This agreement will be in effect for 3 years. It includes the major domestic credit insurers except Euler Hermes.

- The government, through the Compañía Española de Seguro de Crédito a la Exportación (CESCE), has sought to introduce greater flexibility into its ability to support export credit insurance, including the creation of a special facility for providing coverage of "pools" of small and medium-sized firms in association with sectoral associations and chambers of commerce (CESCE-PYME). The government has presented a plan to Parliament that would |

	establish a scheme for the CESCE similar to that for the CCS that would provide coverage of EUR9 billion worth of export credit insurance policies.

(See *Plan E: Plan Español para el Estímulo de la Economía y el Empleo* (Gobierno de España); UNESPA Comunicación of 27 March 2009; Guy Carpenter, *Continental European Legislative and Judicial Trends: Spain*, 18 June 2009; Globedia, "El Consorcio de Seguros y Unespa cubren transacciones de crédito por 20.000 millones en 2009" (2 July 2009); *Negocio*, 22 October 2009; and *Convenio de Reasuguro para el Riesgo de Credito*) |
Switzerland	No known changes or initiatives.
Sweden	No known changes or initiatives except that the overall guarantee limit for state export guarantee agency (EKN) was raised.
Turkey	No known changes or initiatives.
U.K.	The UK government introduced a Trade Credit Insurance Top-up Scheme (TCITS) that became operational in May 2009. The TCITS enables any UK firm with a credit insurance whole-turnover policy that has seen a reduction in its coverage with respect to a particular purchaser to purchase additional insurance with respect to that purchaser. The scheme does not apply to firms that have seen their underlying cover fully removed. The scheme only applies to trades taking place within the UK and thus excludes export transactions. The scheme is administered by the private sector on behalf of the government and will be in place under 31 December 2009, after which no top-up policies will be offered. The aggregate level of top-up insurance provided under the scheme is capped at £5 billion.

Top-up coverage is available if the:

- the underlying cover is in respect of trades taking place within the UK;
- the trades covered by the insurance have payment terms of no more than 120 days, and any pre-shipment coverage included in your underlying policy terms is of no more than 120 days;
- the original level of cover was in place for at least 30 days;
- the reduction in the level of cover happened either on, or after, 1 October 2008; and,
- the reduction in the level of cover was instigated by the credit insurer – and not at the request of the insured.

Up to 28 days' retrospective cover can be purchased in circumstances where a business requires continuity of cover from a partial reduction made by insurers in the previous 28 days.

Top-up policies can be bought under the government scheme for a period of six months. The coverage that can be obtained is the lower of the following amounts:

- the amount that restores the level of cover to the amount previously held;
- the amount equal to the level of cover now offered under the credit insurance policy; or,
- £2 million.

If the underlying cover is full withdrawn, then the top-up cover will be terminated. Transactions already covered will continue to be insured under the top-up scheme, but no new transactions |

	will be covered. *E.g.*:

- If cover provided by the underlying policy is reduced from £100,000 to £80,000 then top-up cover of £20,000 can be purchased to restore cover to the original level of £100,000. If cover subsequently reduces to £50,000, then an additional top-up cover of £30,000 can be purchased, bringing the value of the top-up policy to £50,000, restoring the total level of cover to the original level of £100,000.

- However, if the underlying cover subsequently falls below £50,000, for example to £20,000, then the level of cover provided by the top-up policy will fall to match the amount provided by the underlying policy, in this case £20,000. The total level of cover will therefore be £40,000.

The (six-month) premium rate for top-up cover is 1% of the level of top-up cover provided under the scheme at the time when the firm joined the scheme. An administrative charge is applied by the credit insurers administering the scheme. If the case arise where it is possible to purchase additional top-up coverage, then premium amount will increase (based on extra amount needed and amount of time remaining on the policy). If the underlying cover falls during the first three months, then a refund on the premium paid is possible (1/3 multiplied by the difference between the higher level of cover and the lower level of cover provided under the top-up policy during this period). Beyond three months, no refund is possible.

Firms with top-up cover are permitted to change credit insurers as long as the credit insurer to whom they are transferring their business is also part of the scheme, and disclosure is made of the use of top-up policy. All credit insurers participating in the government scheme adhere to a statement of principles, published by the Association of British Insurers, that outlines the behaviour of credit insurance providers.

Changes have been made to the scheme since its introduction, *e.g.*: backdating of retroactivity to 1 October 2008, instead of 1 April 2009; reducing premium rate from 2% to 1%; abolishing minimum amount of top-up coverage (£20,000); and increasing maximum top-up cover from £1 million to £2 million.

No known changes have been made to the Export Credits Guarantee Department's (ECGD) export credit insurance policy, which is available for transactions valued at more than £20,000 involving capital goods, provision of services, or construction projects (transactions involving consumer goods or commodities on short payment terms are excluded). No coverage is provided for developed country markets.

Additional notes:

– In 2008, credit insurance firms insured over £300 billion of turnover, covering over 14,000 UK clients in transactions with over 250,000 UK businesses.

– As of 2 September, 52 companies had benefited from £1.1 million in coverage (viewed as too low).

(*Government Trade Credit Insurance Top-up Scheme – Product Details*, Department for Business Innovation and Skills, at www.businesslink.gov.uk; UK *Budget 2009*) |
| **U.S.** | In October 2008, the Export-Import Bank of the United States (Ex-Im Bank) reduced its premium rate by 15% on two types of export credit insurance: short-term small business multibuyer policies (designated as ENB), and short-term small business environmental multibuyer policies (designated as ENV). The premium rate reduction, effective Oct. 1, 2008, affects approximately half of all Ex-Im Bank insurance policy holders. |

| | In November 2009, the Ex-Im Bank raised the upper limit of its small business multibuyer export credit insurance policy. The eligibility ceiling was raised from US$5,000,000 to US$7,500,000. Other policy enhancements include: 1) no first loss deductibles, 2) discounted insurance premiums, and 3) the receipt of cost-free, exporter performance risk protection for lenders financing receivables for qualified exporters. The broadened program eligibility will be effective 1 December 2009. Current Ex-Im Bank multibuyer policy holders who previously were ineligible for coverage enhancements but are eligible under the new ceiling, will be offered conversions to the enhanced policy.

(See www.exim.gov) |

ORGANISATION FOR ECONOMIC CO-OPERATION AND DEVELOPMENT

The OECD is a unique forum where governments work together to address the economic, social and environmental challenges of globalisation. The OECD is also at the forefront of efforts to understand and to help governments respond to new developments and concerns, such as corporate governance, the information economy and the challenges of an ageing population. The Organisation provides a setting where governments can compare policy experiences, seek answers to common problems, identify good practice and work to co-ordinate domestic and international policies.

The OECD member countries are: Australia, Austria, Belgium, Canada, Chile, the Czech Republic, Denmark, Estonia, Finland, France, Germany, Greece, Hungary, Iceland, Ireland, Israel, Italy, Japan, Korea, Luxembourg, Mexico, the Netherlands, New Zealand, Norway, Poland, Portugal, the Slovak Republic, Slovenia, Spain, Sweden, Switzerland, Turkey, the United Kingdom and the United States. The European Commission takes part in the work of the OECD.

OECD Publishing disseminates widely the results of the Organisation's statistics gathering and research on economic, social and environmental issues, as well as the conventions, guidelines and standards agreed by its members.